With or Without You

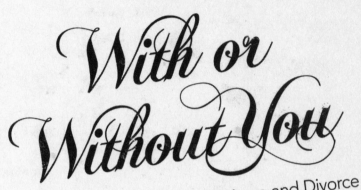

With or Without You

A Spiritual Journey Through Love and Divorce

Cameron Conant

[RELEVANTBOOKS]
WWW.RELEVANTBOOKS.COM

Published by Relevant Books
A division of Relevant Media Group, Inc.

www.relevantbooks.com
www.relevantmediagroup.com

© 2005 Relevant Media Group

Design by Relevant Solutions
Cover design by Greg Leppart
Interior design by Jeremy Kennedy

For information or bulk orders:
RELEVANT MEDIA GROUP, INC.
100 SOUTH LAKE DESTINY DR., STE 200
ORLANDO, FL 32810
407-660-1411

Library of Congress Control Number: 2005902187
International Standard Book Number: 0-9763642-7-1

05 06 07 08 09 8 7 6 5 4 3 2 1

Printed in the United States of America

CONTENTS

Preface   vii
Acknowledgments   xi

Chapter 1 - The Shaky Beginning of a Dream   1

Chapter 2 - Walking Toward Something   17

Chapter 3 - Engagement   33

Chapter 4 - Celebrate with Us?   41

Chapter 5 - All That You Can't Leave Behind   53

Chapter 6 - A Bad Moment   69

Chapter 7 - Losing Myself   85

Chapter 8 - Alone in the World   101

Chapter 9 - Look Straight Ahead   111

Chapter 10 - The Last Night and First Weeks   125

Chapter 11 - Death   137

Chapter 12 - Wrestling with God and Demons   153

Chapter 13 - Evil, Love, and Grace   183

Chapter 14 - Visitation   195

Chapter 15 - Day Three   203

Notes   207

Preface

When I was about twelve, my mischievous aunt found a Tony the Tiger bumper sticker in a cereal box. It looked ridiculous—and she knew it—which is why she plastered Tony to the back of our Chrysler minivan. When my father saw it, he was upset and spent hours in the driveway trying to remove Tony. Despite his efforts, remnants of the sticker were still there. Pieces of Tony the Tiger were permanently stuck to the minivan.

Like that bumper sticker, pieces of me are permanently stuck to something—or someone. Nothing can reattach parts of my life that once seemed permanently glued together. But my situation is more than an irritating bumper sticker. It's emotional. It's spiritual. It's physical.

I'm divorced.

My divorce has impacted my life more than any other single event, yet in some ways I'm still not used to saying it, writing it, or even talking about it. As I write this book, I'm twenty-seven. I come from a good family. I go to church. I believe in God. I have a good job. But none of that stopped my wife from leaving. None of that stopped me from feeling like a failure. None of that stopped the sadness that came in tsunami waves after my wife left.

Part of me is forever stuck to my ex-wife, and in my own way, I'm like my father standing in the driveway: scrubbing, scrubbing, scrubbing, hoping to make the spoiled pristine. But the mark remains. It's there for all to see—a part of my history, a part of my present.

This book is part of my attempt to make sense of what happened to me and, in so doing, perhaps make some sense of what's happened to you or to someone you care about. But first, a warning: This is going to be ugly, and because of that, I don't want to write this. But something tells me that I must.

I Thought You Should Know

Before you begin this book, I feel a strange obligation to tell you several things. Perhaps some of them are obvious, perhaps some are less so.

First of all, I have found it necessary to alter some names, dates, places, and times in order to protect the identities of people who wouldn't want to be identified. My publisher even asked that I consider writing this book under a pseudonym, which I considered but ultimately decided against.

I decided against it because I felt that it was important to attach my real name to this story. There is something liberating about that; by using my real name, I'm telling you that I refuse to live the rest of my life in shame, that I refuse to hide from the past, that I refuse to hide from the responsibility that comes from putting things down on paper.

You should also know that I have not tried to sanitize this story. It is raw, and intentionally so. I wanted to convey the hurt, pain, and confusion that I felt during this difficult time in my life.

Many wise people have counseled me while I wrote this book. I have sought their counsel for several reasons. I never wanted to write something that was an exercise in bitterness or self-loathing; I wanted to write something that others would find helpful, at least in some mysterious, God-ordained way. A friend who is divorced told me, "Write two versions of the story; one for only you and God to see and one for the rest of us to read. We will all be better off for it." I thought his advice was wise, and I have tried to do as he suggested.

In fact, I never wanted to write something that would hurt my ex-wife, and the idea that this book could hurt her gave me pause and forced me to reread the entire manuscript after it was completed, carefully combing through the story line by line to make sure that my portrayal of her (and of myself) was as accurate as a one-sided account could be.

I also want you to know this: I cannot escape the fact that this book was written less than one year after my wife left and filed for divorce, which means I have not had the luxury of years of perspective. Instead, this book is a snapshot in time, and writing it has been a journey of self-discovery—a journey that I invite you to join. As you take this journey with me, you will find (again, returning to the rawness) that I refuse to gloss over the pain, confusion, and sadness that accompany divorce.

I refuse to downplay these things because I am too close to them. I refuse to give easy answers to difficult questions because I have lived far too long with trite axioms to complex problems. I agree with John Steinbeck, who once asked, "How many people have seen or heard or felt something that so outraged their sense of what should be that the whole thing was brushed quickly away like dirt under a rug? For myself, I try to keep that line open even for things I can't understand or explain ... "[1]

I hope that my story will help you keep that line open for things that you can't understand or explain. And in keeping that line open, I hope that you will feel with me, because my intent is not so much to explain as it is to feel, to experience something holy in the midst of something so unholy.

Though this story is far from a Sunday school lesson, I hope that it will somehow convey the most profound truth in history: that Jesus loves us—much better than anyone else ever will, much better than we will ever love ourselves.

Acknowledgments

Thanks go to Cara Davis at Relevant Books for your belief
in this story and, by extension, your belief in me. Jeff Jackson
and Cameron Strang at Relevant Books for your support and
encouragement. Shari VandenBerg and Ben Irwin of Zondervan: Not only are you incredible editors, but incredible people
as well. Your encouragement, enthusiasm, and editorial skill will
forever be appreciated. The many friends who have stood by
me and loved me when I needed it the most, especially Rob
Stewart, Melinda Van Kirk, Leslie (Pratt) Speyers, Kim Zeilstra,
Sarah Buter, Aaron Carriere, Jon Petersen, Derek VanderWeide,
and Alex Reineking. My former colleagues at Zondervan for
making work a refuge in the midst of emotional pain, particularly Paul Caminiti, Brad Doll, Vicki Cessna, Mark Rice, Karen
Campbell, and Becky Cowan. My former teacher, Mary Groom,
for believing in an unmotivated sixteen-year-old kid. My
parents, Dennis and Jana, for showing me the way; my brother,
Christian, and sister, Alissa, for loving me. Rob Lacey, Renee
Altson, and Bill and Rachel Taylor-Beales for reminding me of

the holy power of art and story. Jeff Buursma, to whom I can only say, "I was a stranger, you took me in." Rick Van Grouw, who taught me journalism and, perhaps more importantly, put up with me in my fundamentalist days. Paige Harvey, for her friendship and encouragement; Schuler Books and Music in Grand Rapids, Michigan—my favorite bookstore and the place where I wrote much of this book. To the people who know how it feels to hit rock bottom; to the music of U2, which mends my soul in ways I will never fully understand; and most importantly, to the ongoing story of God, which is unfolding in my life and yours.

Kurie eleison, Christe eleison, Kurie eleison.

Lord have mercy, Christ have mercy, Lord have mercy.

A Word About Memories
Memories live in a world of their own.
They are tied to reality, but separate from it;
they are part fact and part fiction.
They are part of our mind's attempt
to make sense of something that doesn't.

Memories are our past.

Memories are our future.

You are about to read my memories.

Chapter One

The Shaky Beginning of a Dream

Let's see colors that have never been seen
Let's go places no one else has been
You're in my mind all of the time

—"Electrical Storm," U2

She was beautiful.

Not movie-star beautiful, but girl-next-door beautiful. A friend said she looked like a Precious Moments doll—big eyes, angelic face, beautiful hair. A sort of sweetness radiated from her.

I first saw her during my freshman year of college. I noticed the beautiful girls right away—only 1,300 students attended my Midwestern liberal arts college—but I was only interested in her. I'll call her Sara.

I don't remember much about the first time I saw Sara, but I remember going back to my dorm room, scanning a book of freshman photographs that the college gave us. I finally found her picture.

Something about her chin made me smile. It protruded strangely from her face, but it was more endearing than odd. With a yellow highlighter, I circled her picture. I couldn't figure out what it was that attracted me to her—there were plenty of beautiful women who should've warranted just as much attention from my overactive hormones—but there was something about her.

There was only one problem: I was dating Mary. Five months earlier, Mary and I had gone to our high school prom together. At the time we were just friends, but as spring turned to summer, we began spending more time together. Soon things evolved into an unspoken romance.

Mary was tall and lanky and wonderful, the sort of person who always thought of others first. Once Mary and I were kissing when my jaw suddenly locked. For about three minutes, I was humiliated as my mouth was open wide enough for small birds to have nested there. But Mary didn't laugh—in fact, she never told anyone. That's the kind of person Mary was.

Our relationship ended when I stopped writing her during my freshman year of college, soon before email became as common as telephones. Mary's handwritten letters—sent to my dorm room—began to pile up, and my responses became shorter and shorter, and then stopped altogether.

I was an arrogant jerk, but I tried not to think about that. I also tried not to think about Mary, and it worked. Sara took her place, though she had done nothing to warrant such attention.

It must have been pure attraction, yet it seemed so much more than that—at least to my eighteen-year-old mind. I sensed that Sara was good, pure, and sweet, which explains why I made the following proclamation to the guys in my college residence hall.

"See this girl," I said with bravado, pointing to Sara's picture. "I'm going to date her."

Cheers and high-fives and jokes abounded. Bets were made. I was on a mission.

But little did I know where my mission would take me; little did I know that I was headed for a train wreck that would change my life forever. In search of something good—something better—I would find something altogether different, something I would have never predicted.

The First Call

I called her dorm room, and she answered. After a joke or two, we laughed awkwardly. She hardly knew me.

Weeks earlier, I asked her to go to a movie with me—*Braveheart*—and she declined, saying that she was going to be out of town. She was too sweet to tell me that she had a boyfriend. Now that I had finally called her, she had to tell me the truth. She had to tell me about a song she was practicing in her voice class.

The song was in German.

She was learning the song for her boyfriend who spoke German.

When I heard "boyfriend," my chest deflated, my mouth went dry, my stomach hurt. I wanted to end the conversation right away, but my pride wouldn't let me. I tried to act as if I wasn't interested in her, tried to act as if I was calling as a friend. But it was too late: I was caught red-handed. Sara knew I was interested in more than friendship.

I wanted to have a *Groundhog Day* moment and reverse time, perhaps never to have picked up the phone at all. But after recovering from my humiliation, a resolve—the same resolve I felt when elbowed in the heat of a basketball game—rose to the surface.

I was determined to pick myself up, dive for the ball, elbow back. I wasn't about to lose to a guy who was attending a business college in New York, a guy who spoke German and came from a wealthy family, a guy who seemed to have it all together, a guy who was everything I wasn't.

Sara had dated this German-speaking boyfriend through the latter part of high school. From the way she talked about him, it was clear that their relationship was serious.

I wasn't deterred.

I began looking for Sara around campus, finding her in the library, asking if I could sit across from her, teasing her about a winter hat that she wore. Soon, we were laughing in corners of lecture halls and on park benches.

We were only friends, but as we began spending more time together, I began hearing less and less about the German-speaking boyfriend. I was convinced that this was not only a good thing for me, but a good thing for Sara as well.

Sara made very few friends the first semester of our freshman year. As she felt more and more alone, she began to retreat inward, living only for daily phone calls to her mom and her boyfriend. Someone had to pull her out of this—I wanted to be that someone.

Years later, Sara told me that if it hadn't been for my friendship, she would have left and transferred to another school.

I'm not sure that Sara had ever made friends easily, but that first semester, she didn't want to make friends. Sara was very comfortable with her friends from high school, very comfortable with her boyfriend. In fact, she almost seemed to feel that she was betraying her high school friends by developing a new circle of friends in college.

Sara was usually gone on the weekends—visiting her boyfriend, her family, her high school friends. If she stayed on campus, she spent Friday nights in her dorm room, typing away on her computer—books sprawled out all over her desk—obsessing over a four-page paper as if anything less than an "A" would result in a swift execution.

Sara was the classic overachiever. She was in college to study—and study hard. She was bright, but she had to work hard for her grades. And her hard work paid off. She rarely, if ever, attained anything less than a 3.8 GPA.

Sara told childhood stories of "required reading time" at home, stories of having to do "school homework" assignments and then "mom's homework" assignments. This helped me understand the desperation with which she tackled her course work.

The fact that Sara and I were seemingly attracted to each other either made perfect sense or no sense at all. We were complete opposites. I made friends easily—always had. I was voted to the homecoming court by the student body at my preppy Catholic high school. People felt like they knew me—liked me—even if, in reality, they didn't really know me at all.

If Sara was the classic overachiever, I was perhaps the classic underachiever. I remember high school math and science teachers shaking their heads, pulling me aside after class, asking me why I scored so poorly on this test or that quiz. I remember failed attempts at keeping a day planner, mediocre grades even in subjects that came naturally to me, such as English or history. I remember having to repeat high school algebra, feeling like one of the "dumb" students as I—a junior—sat in a classroom full of sophomores. I remember barely getting into the college of my choice because of my less-than-stellar grades. I even had to be interviewed by a college admissions counselor before the school would accept me as a student.

Sara and I made an odd pair.

We Were Only Freshmen

Sara was still dating the German-speaker when she returned to school after Christmas break, but she was never far from my thoughts.

As winter turned to spring, Sara announced that she and the German-speaker were taking a hiatus from their relationship. I was shocked and excited. One day, I handed Sara a bouquet of flowers as she studied in an old lecture hall. She threw her arms around me.

Our relationship quickly became intense—phone calls, notes, weekends together, afternoons in the library, glances over the tops of books. One day, Sara asked if I wanted to be her date for a friend's wedding. I would be able to meet her parents and her high school friends and get away from campus for a weekend.

I vaguely remember the visit to Sara's house. Looking at a picture taken in Sara's living room just before we left for the wedding helps—Sara looking so young, wearing a yellow dress … me looking even younger, wearing khaki pants, a tie, and one of my dad's navy-blue sport coats.

I remember being quiet—so anxious to make a good impression on Sara's family and friends, so hesitant to open up and be myself, afraid that I might not be good enough. Despite my anxiety, the visit painted a fuller picture of who Sara was. I'm not sure you can fully understand someone without first observing their family. And this was my first chance to see that part of Sara's life.

Meeting the Family

The house was a two-story brick home with white siding, just around the corner from Sara's old middle school. It was firmly ensconced in suburbia. Case in point: It looked like virtually every house around it—basketball hoop in the driveway, perfectly manicured front lawn. It had a small backyard with a wooden fence, which protected a swimming pool and water slide. Inside, the house looked like an Ethan Allen showroom, with expensive furniture, tasteful paintings, and a La-Z-Boy chair reserved for Sara's father.

Her father—tall, thin, athletic—was a quiet man who kept to himself. He seemed to carry some deep pain around with him. He was always tinkering in the basement or golfing or inspecting something in the backyard.

Sara's brother—only two years younger—was something of a genius. He was very smart, political, and outspoken on economic and social issues. And like his father, he was quiet around those he didn't know—that is, until politics were mentioned. Her youngest brother, a skateboarder, constantly had punk music blaring from his room. He was four years younger than Sara and was the most talkative and outgoing of the family. Sara's sister was six years younger—the baby of the family. She was creative, sweet, and quiet.

The first time I visited Sara's house, I slept in her room, on the floor in a sleeping bag. I always found it strange that her parents allowed this—no, actually encouraged it. I didn't tell my parents, knowing they wouldn't approve. I didn't care. I was old enough to make my own decisions. I was eighteen and learning what it meant to take responsibility for my own actions, or so I told myself.

I judged Sara's family harshly. They were anything but "good" evangelicals like most of the people I knew. They didn't pray before meals or have any Bibles lying around. Sara's younger siblings were allowed to watch MTV. Her dad listened to Madonna. They let their daughter have a guy—me—sleep in her bedroom. They had an ample supply of beer and wine in the house. All of these things were a bit taboo for the Baptists I grew up around.

Even so, it was strange that these things bothered me. I liked people of faith—respected them—but I wasn't sure I was one. Nevertheless, I developed all of the exteriors: a good "church face," all the right answers to the big questions, and the ability to lead a prayer with the best of them. I was also pretty good at judging people.

The Past

Sara's mom, Kate, had a difficult childhood. Her father died shortly after he returned from World War II, leaving Kate's mother to raise Kate and her three siblings alone. Kate's mom became an alcoholic, which didn't mesh well with the full-time job she took in order to support the family. The family didn't have much. Kate sewed her own clothes and worked her way through Catholic high school.

Kate married and had children young. In fact, she ended up being the only one of her three siblings to produce children. She wore this as a badge of pride, along with her ability to keep her marriage intact.

Kate saw the world in black and white. She loved passionately, and she hated passionately. Sometimes she wouldn't speak to Sara's dad for days at a time. She loved her children unlike any parent I've ever seen. She ironed their clothes, made virtually every meal, cleaned bedrooms, did laundry, and more.

I knew much less about Sara's dad and his history. He was a third-generation Italian but lost his father as a small child growing up in the Midwest. Losing his father at such an early age seemed to haunt Sara's dad.

There was always tension when I was with Sara's family, even after Sara and I were married. Perhaps they sensed my judgmental attitude. Or perhaps the tension came from the fact that we were so different from each other and didn't share the same interests, ideas, and backgrounds.

I suspect that it was a combination of all of these things, along with the fact that there was a strange bunker mentality that existed in the home. Everything was about the family: protecting the family, being with the family, being absolutely devoted to the family. Few people ever made their way inside—boyfriends and girlfriends came and went. Sara's parents didn't have any real community. They had only a few adult friends, and they both came from families on the verge of extinction. Their whole identity was wrapped up in their family. And years later, this family would begin to crumble.

Breaking Up

The breakup came in the late spring of my freshman year, just weeks before college ended for the summer. Sara said something about needing some space, needing time to think.

I was devastated, perhaps even more so because I was in a one-act play with Sara on campus. The play was horrible, both artistically and personally. Sara and I had to dance and kiss. I remember whispering something overly dramatic and silly to her during one performance after we had broken up: "Well, this might be the last time we ever dance."

That wasn't true. We would dance again, but it would take some time. We went our separate ways that summer, but she had a hold on me. There were plenty of late nights that July and August, sitting at the desk in my bedroom, a fluorescent light shining directly on me, combing through Shakespeare's sonnets at two in the morning. One of my favorites that I carefully transcribed in a letter to Sara was "Sonnet 27":

Weary with toil, I haste me to my bed,
The dear repose for limbs with travel tired;
But then begins a journey in my head
To work my mind, when body's work's expired;
For then my thoughts, from far where I abide,
Intend a zealous pilgrimage to thee,
And keep my drooping eyelids open wide,
Looking on darkness which the blind do see:
Save that my soul's imaginary sight
Presents thy shadow to my sightless view,
Which, like a jewel hung in ghastly night,
Makes black night beauteous and her old face new.
Lo, thus, by day my limbs, by night my mind
For thee, and for myself, no quiet find.[1]

I later learned that this letter and others like it had a profound impact on Sara. But when I returned to college for my sophomore year, our roles switched. I had started to give up on Sara; she had started to give in to me.

Drunk Love

I returned for my sophomore year with a chip on my shoulder. Part of me still wanted a relationship with Sara, but I was hurt—angry about how I had been treated. I don't remember ever telling her this directly, but I certainly communicated it indirectly. About two months into the semester, Sara came to me, telling me how she felt, telling me she wanted to get back together. I was studying in the college library.

"I really value your friendship, Sara, which is why I think we should just be friends," I said. It seemed a nice answer, but it was really borne out of deep hurt, resentment, and anger.

As so often happens in relationships, the more Sara wanted me, the less I felt that I needed her. The strange thing is that I don't remember what it was that reunited us. I suppose it was the simple fact that I missed her and still cared about her. We were dating again by the time I was inducted into my college's theater honorary that spring.

The night I was inducted was a night that I'll never forget. I auditioned with a monologue, a blinding spotlight trained on my head. After all of the inductees were finished, we took the secret pledge and were done for the night. Or so I thought.

To my surprise, there was a second part of the initiation: a party at the president's house. Though it was a weeknight and I had a major exam the next day, I didn't protest as I was led to the house. Shortly after I arrived, the alcohol began flowing. Beer. Wine. Liquor. I began drinking ... and drinking ... and drinking.

Sitting on an old, discolored couch, I felt warm and happy and strangely willing to say or do anything. At nineteen, this was the second time in my life I had been drunk. But this time, I was truly out of control. The evening wore on toward midnight, and then past midnight. I started kissing a girl who was a friend of mine, then I kissed another.

I ended up calling my roommate to pick me up. I was standing in the front yard of this house, pale-faced, ready to vomit as he pulled up at about 2:30 a.m. I missed the test that I was supposed to take the next day. I told people that I was sick, not hung over. I spent the day in bed, frequently running to the community bathroom to throw up.

I never told Sara this happened, even though we were dating at the time.

"Dude, it's okay. You were drunk," a friend told me when I expressed concern about what happened that evening. "Yes, he's right. I was drunk," I thought. "Not that big of a deal."

I had grown up in the church, but I was far from a follower of Jesus. In fact, I never admitted it, but I wondered if the entire story of Jesus wasn't just a fairy tale that people believed to help them fall asleep at night. I guess that's one reason why I was able to dismiss my conscience so easily. A few months later, I had even more practice dismissing my conscience. My friend and I went to Cancun, Mexico, for spring break. While there, our Mexican host had us go on the "Booze Cruise." "You'll love it," he said with a thick Mexican accent. "You must do it."

We did. I ended up drinking too much and kissing some girl from Chattanooga. Again, I never told Sara. But it was okay. I was drunk.

Bad Hair and Other Problems

Sara deserved better than me—at least better than the nineteen-year-old me. She was always supportive, and I was so needy.

Like when I started losing my hair—or so I thought. The winter of my sophomore year, I was sicker than I had ever been ... on the verge of pneumonia, in bed for several days. My friends were my lifeline. They brought soup and saltines and sandwiches. My roommate brought medicine.

Shortly after Christmas, whether it was a result of the illness I'm not sure, I started losing what felt like clumps of hair. I was terrified. My self-esteem took a nose dive every time I climbed in the shower and saw the amount of hair coming out of my head.

I began retreating inward, spending time in the basement of the college library, sulking, reading through medical journals. I visited my uncle who was a doctor. I bought special shampoo. I suppose it is a testament to how shallow I was that something like this could've bothered me so much, but it did. And Sara bore the brunt of my depression.

"Will you still love me if I lose my hair?" I would ask her, only half-joking.

"Of course I will—and you're not losing your hair, so stop saying that. It looks fine," Sara would say, a grin peeking out of the corner of her mouth.

I loved Sara, but I didn't believe her. I thought I looked terrible. I imagined I was only days away from looking like a guy in my dorm whose hairline started halfway up his skull. My depression lingered, even after it appeared that I wouldn't go bald anytime soon. I can only imagine the sort of draining effect that I had on Sara—Saturday nights sulking, Wednesday afternoons questioning my worth and begging for her to fill me with something she couldn't.

I was a prisoner of my own questions and self-doubt. I had always struggled with self-image, vacillating between arrogance and deep questions of self-worth. I suppose the hair loss simply reminded me of past demons.

The depression lasted through spring and on into the summer, when I landed a role in a regional Shakespeare festival. It was my first professional acting gig. I made a whopping $250 for about two months of work.

I was starting to come out of my depression; acting had that effect on me. I was a decent actor, but I wondered if I didn't do it because it fed my fragile ego. I sometimes wondered if my favorite moments were the curtain calls, the hand-shaking afterward, the awards. And now that I had landed two roles in two of the festival's plays—albeit small roles—my confidence spiked.

Unfortunately, it was too late. Shortly after I started rehearsal, Sara told me that she needed a break. She was exhausted—likely, tired of putting up with me. And I couldn't blame her.

Gone Again

I was upset, but fortunately, it didn't send me spiraling back into depression. It was probably because I was so busy that summer. In addition to performing in the Shakespeare festival, I was performing in Scotland's Fringe Festival in a play directed by my college theater professor. I was also planning a trip to the East Coast and Canada with friends.

While traveling that summer, I remember lying on a hotel bed in Niagara Falls after doing a shot of liquor, saying that if I ever got another chance with Sara, I wouldn't blow it, that if I got another chance, I would marry her. Sara was the only one for me—or so I had convinced myself. Of course, I really had only dated one other girl in my life—and that was when I was in high school.

My heart felt as if it was constantly breaking as each day passed without Sara. I was always wondering how she was doing, what she was doing, and whether she was dating anyone new. As we moved east on our road trip and headed into Montreal that summer, I remember buying Sara a postcard there, trying not to sound too desperate as I filled virtually every square inch with my handwriting.

Two weeks later, aboard an overnight flight to England, I thought of Sara as I drank the small bottles of wine that they provided to twenty-year-olds over international air space. I'm not sure why I never accepted defeat, why it didn't occur to me that we simply weren't meant for each other. But it never did. I was persistent, perhaps to a fault.

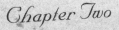

Chapter Two

Walking Toward Something

Home ... hard to know what it is
if you've never had one
Home ... I can't say where it is
but I know I'm going home
That's where the hurt is

—"Walk On," U2

I spent my junior year of college living in a house that my
roommates and I called "The Highlands." The name was chosen
in honor of *Braveheart*—the epic film about Scottish hero William Wallace, played by Mel Gibson. We named our dog Sir
Robert the Bruce after the legendary Scottish nobleman, also
portrayed in the movie.

Only blocks from campus, The Highlands was quite possibly the perfect college house. It was big enough for parties, and the rent was reasonable. I was also surrounded by friends, which helped ease the pain of life without Sara. Despite having friends around me, I still wondered when the empty pit in my stomach would be filled, when I would stop hurting, when I would be able to walk around campus without worrying about Sara. In fact, I replayed one scenario in my mind over and over again: seeing Sara in the cafeteria, acting like I didn't care, laughing with my friends as I passed her, basically doing anything to convey that life was great without her—even if it wasn't.

A few weeks into the semester I went to a fraternity party with a friend. I knew that Sara would be there because the sorority she had recently pledged was cosponsoring the event. The scene was typical: loud music, a crowded house, drunken people, preppy frat guys with too much cologne, party girls with tight clothes and bleached blonde hair. There were bodies on couches, bodies on steps, bodies on the dance floor.

As soon as I saw Sara, I felt lightheaded. Catching glimpses of her between flailing arms and beer cans, I wondered who she was talking to, what she was thinking, who she was watching. Did she miss me? Did she even think about me? It had been weeks since we last spoke.

One of my first days on campus that semester, I had given Sara some stationery that I bought in Scotland. She loved stationery. As we talked, it was clear that she wasn't prepared to start dating again. And so I avoided any contact with her.

But when I saw her that night, I wanted to make her angry. I wanted her to feel the way I did—sad, angry, confused, frustrated. Karaoke had just started, which gave me an idea: Maybe I could sing a song that would upset Sara. The more I thought about it, the more I liked the idea. After looking at the playlist, I found the perfect song: "Separate Lives" by Phil Collins. It was a duet, and my friend sang the female part—I made sure of that. Despite the obvious humor inherent in the song (I believe VH1 included "Separate Lives" in its list of all-time "Awesomely Bad Duets"), the words were intended to jab Sara right in the gut. "You have no right to ask me how I feel," we sang.

My plan worked. As we finished the song, someone told me that Sara was fuming.

We're Not Dating

Late that first semester of our junior year, Sara and I began talking to each other again, though I don't remember why. We still liked each other, yet there was so much hurt, so much frustration lurking just beneath the surface. Sara was going to be leaving soon for a semester abroad, so we decided that dating was a bad idea for the time being.

Before Sara left for Europe, we agreed that we would continue talking on the phone to determine if we wanted to date when she returned. It was frustrating to know that just as things were moving toward "us," we were being pulled apart by Sara's semester in Europe. Neither of us felt angry—studying abroad had been a dream of Sara's for years—but we both felt sad knowing we would be separated by an ocean for more than four months.

"Well, I'll miss you," I said over the phone only one day before Sara left. "I don't know what's going to happen, but I'll miss you."

"I'll miss you, too," Sara said. "Maybe we'll know where things are headed when I return."

As Sara prepared to leave, I was faced with a decision: Sara or Lisa. Of course, Sara didn't know that I was being faced with such a decision—in fact no one knew, except for one of my roommates. Months earlier when Sara was still uninterested in dating, I started spending time with Lisa. Lisa and I usually hung out in big groups. But once, we went to dinner together—just the two of us. Another time, I took Lisa to the doctor when she was sick. And now, just as Sara was leaving for Europe, Lisa and I started talking to each other on the phone.

Lisa was quite possibly the sweetest girl I had ever met. She reminded me of my mom—good natured, agreeable, a great smile, smart, and always slightly unsure of herself.

As Sara prepared to leave for the semester, I weighed all of the pros and cons between her and Lisa. I intuitively knew that I was at a crossroads. I envisioned one road leading to a life with Sara, and the other, a life with Lisa. I wondered what those two lives would be like, how they would compare to one another. Yet when it came right down to deciding, I was in too deep. I wasn't strong enough to even consider someone other than Sara.

I suppose I always knew that I would choose Sara because she had such a strong pull on me. In fact, even making the most intractable mistake with Sara seemed better than not trying at all. What I didn't realize was that intractable mistakes hurt like hell.

Valentine's Day

With an international calling card, I phoned Sara as frequently as possible that semester. We also exchanged emails and handwritten letters. We missed each other, but perhaps never more than on Valentine's Day. Before Instant Messenger became commonplace, there was only email, which we both happened to be doing at the same time that evening. Sitting in the college computer lab after dinner with a few dateless friends, I received an email from her only moments after sending one. Furiously, I typed another, asking her if she was currently on the computer. About two minutes later, an email came back from her with nine exclamation points, stating that she too was emailing me at that very moment. It was something of a Valentine's Day miracle, 1997 style.

I wish I could say that something happened that evening that changed the nature of my relationship with Sara forever, that confirmed my love for her. But that wouldn't be true. I loved Sara long before that night in the computer lab. In fact, I sometimes wondered if I had always loved her.

A Long Embrace

Our relationship intensified as the semester drew to a close. We knew we were prepared to date again, and we could hardly wait to see each other. Naturally, I jumped at the chance to pick Sara up at the airport late that spring. Pacing back and forth outside of the terminal, I waited at the airport more than an hour before Sara's flight from London even landed. As she walked into the terminal (finally), my face lit up. She looked stunning. She was wearing a short sundress, and her light brown hair—punctuated by natural streaks of blonde—looked beautiful.

We quickly walked toward each other—a notch below jogging—and embraced. "I missed you so much," I said. "I missed you, too," Sara said. We both had tears in our eyes. I had never been happier to see someone. As we held each other, I noticed how soft Sara's skin was, how good she smelled, how I wanted to be with her forever. We seemed to grip each other tighter and tighter, as if both of us were afraid to ever let go again. As we held each other, I thought of how Sara taught me how to hug.

During our freshman year my hugs were weak and done with alligator arms—that is until Sara taught me how to really hug, how to fully embrace someone. Her hugs were executed with textbook form: She would hold me close and fully wrap her arms around me. She would then firmly apply pressure with both of her hands to different parts of my back.

As we stood there in the airport, Sara sniffling as tears streamed down her cheeks, I felt her hands pressing against my back, and I realized that home wasn't a place, it was a person. With Sara, I had finally found a home. And I was happy.

Weeks later, we were talking on the phone when the word "marriage" was mentioned for the first time. "I wonder where things are headed with us," I said. "I mean, I wonder if we might get married someday."

"Yeah, I wonder," Sara said. "I think we might."

An Unlikely Counselor

Home from college, I couldn't find anything to do that summer—in part because I didn't want to try my hand at anything too risky or difficult. Waiting tables? I'd never done it and didn't particularly want to try. Construction? I did it one summer and was miserable. Retail? I tried, but couldn't get anything.

Finally, at my mom's prompting, I applied to be a counselor at a Christian summer camp. I would've rather done just about anything else. Suddenly waiting tables looked exciting, mainly because I wasn't comfortable being labeled as a Christian or talking about faith. I didn't really have a faith. Sure, I had thirteen years' worth of Christian schooling: felt boards at my Lutheran grade school with images of Martin Luther nailing his ninety-five theses on the church door at Wittenberg, memories of long-winded talks about the mistakes of Vatican II at my Catholic high school, peppy praise services held by evangelicals at my liberal arts college. But real faith? No. A real desire to know and follow Jesus? No.

Arriving at the rural camp, which was a few miles away from the college I attended, I was given an application to fill out and a tour by Eric, the camp director. I feigned interest as my mind wandered. Finally at the end of the tour, Eric said, "Well, that's it. I guess I should tell you that we have one final opening on our summer staff, and it's for a male counselor. I had a couple of really good candidates in the other day, but after praying about it, I didn't feel like either of them were the right ones for the job. I think you might be the one I'm looking for. I'll look over your resume and give you a call."

I was surprised. Me? I'm the right one for the job? Why? What did I do? How could I be the right one for the job? A week later, Eric called and told me that I made the cut: I was the final staff member. I would be in charge of a cabin each week. Some weeks the campers would be high school students, other weeks, elementary or middle school students. I would also have to lead Bible lessons for my cabin, which was something that terrified me.

This Is for You
Each week a speaker or musician (often the speaker was the musician) came to camp to lead chapel services, which were

held several times per day. The chapel services were often Christian versions of high school pep rallies, which I would tolerate with a mixture of amusement and uneasiness. Sometimes the songs were so cheesy that my stomach became queasy, especially when one or more of my fellow counselors would do hand motions as we sang. It was during those moments that I was terrified of ever being labeled a Christian.

But sometimes the chapel services were more meaningful. It was during these times that I felt as if I were one of the campers and not one of the counselors. During these times my knowledge of the Bible—accumulated over years of Christian schooling—seemed inadequate. Despite my knowledge, I felt virtually nothing. The only thing that I felt was this sense that I didn't really believe any of it. And I couldn't understand how anyone could believe any of it.

Part of my problem was that I never understood the Bible as a story that had anything to do with me—I only understood the Bible as a series of cold statements about theology. That changed one evening when our speaker for the week, John, showed us scenes from *Braveheart*. He compared the suffering that William Wallace endured in the movie to the suffering that Jesus endured on the cross.

I remember fighting back the tears as I sat among a sea of high school campers. There was nothing John said that proved the existence of God, nothing he said that proved that Jesus actually died—let alone, proved that Jesus actually died to forgive me for all of the horrible things I had done. Yet almost inexplicably, I believed. For the first time, I believed. It made no sense to believe, yet in that moment, sometime around nine o'clock on a summer night at a camp in the middle of nowhere, I knew that Jesus was real.

Am I Supposed to Be Better?

Life didn't suddenly change after my spiritual experience. I
didn't start singing hymns or being nice to everyone. Yet something was different. The change was small at first: I started
thinking of all the ways that God was bigger than I was; I started
reading the Bible with fresh eyes; and perhaps most startling, I
started feeling guilty about things I did that I knew were wrong.

This was probably the most annoying part about following
Jesus. I didn't want to change. I was so comfortable with my bad
habits. The fact that I couldn't become the person I needed to
be ate away at me. And if I couldn't change, then I wondered
if I really wanted to be more like Jesus; I began to wonder if I
really had a life-changing experience at all or if I was just being
particularly emotional that evening when the speaker talked
about Jesus.

I didn't realize that faith was a journey. I didn't realize that faith
was only the first step. It would take years for me to realize that
I didn't have to be perfect—I just had to be honest about the
fact that I wasn't.

Sending Letters

I missed Sara terribly that summer. Fortunately, I was able to
see her nearly every weekend, but during the week our com-
munication was limited to handwritten letters. I would sit in
my bunk and pen letters to Sara late into the night as my body
stuck to my hot sleeping bag. My right hand would try to hold
the flashlight steady as my left hand scrawled out sentence after
sentence.

Each day during camp, letters were handed out before dinner,
and I was the primary recipient. Sara's letters were always stuffed

with glitter and written in her beautiful penmanship. Several times, she even sent care packages filled with candy and cards and anything else she could think of to cheer me up. I was so sad without her, but her letters were a welcome retreat from the daylong grind of camp life. Reading her letters, I was transported to a place where breezes blew and campers didn't complain or puke, where life consisted of looking into Sara's blue eyes.

As I read Sara's letters, I was also learning about the changes that were happening in her heart. She was working at a camp that summer too—a Christian day camp for kids from rough backgrounds. That summer, Sara began learning more about Jesus, exploring her own faith, and putting it into action by loving kids who could be pretty unlovable. We both were having spiritual experiences at the same time. I thought it was providence.

The Dance That Broke My Heart

Back at school for my senior year, the fraternities and sororities held a Greek Week event that I attended one evening. Sara and a dozen other girls from her sorority were dancing. The song that they danced to was so loud, I not only heard it, I felt it.

Standing forty yards from the outdoor stage, I could see Sara clearly. I didn't want to be too close, but I wanted to be close enough to watch her. I was protective of her and probably more than a little jealous. If Sara hadn't been involved in the festivities, I would have been as far away from Greek Week as possible. The Greek scene always made me nauseous, perhaps because I knew that fraternity guys were just as evil as I was. You always hate in others what you hate most about yourself. And there was plenty to hate about myself at that time.

Sara was wearing tight black pants and shaking her body to the pulse of the music. I was uneasy, but the song was almost over, and it looked like things would be fine. Suddenly toward the end of the song, one of the fraternity guys—baseball cap on backward—jumped on stage and started dancing. My heart felt as if it might explode as I saw him move toward Sara.

Before I could even think about what was happening, he was gyrating to the music with Sara, and she gyrated back. Their bodies—touching, or nearly so—moved for what seemed like minutes. The crowd screamed their approval, and I felt myself gasping for air. I quickly slipped into the night, sad, angry, and humiliated.

I walked back to my room. After lying on my bed for a few minutes, I became restless. I left the house, aimlessly walking down dark sidewalks in search of something. I found myself stopping at the room of a friend who was a Christian. I told him what had happened and asked him to pray with me. We prayed. We talked. And thirty minutes later, I walked back to my room.

Soon after I returned, Sara knocked on the door. She knew that I was upset before she even saw me. "Where were you? I've been trying to find you for the past hour," she said. "I knew you must have been upset."

"I went for a walk. I had to get away. Yes, I was—am—upset," I said.

We talked about what happened for two hours. "I didn't know what else to do," Sara said. "When he came toward me, what was I supposed to do? Turn away? I'm sorry ... I really didn't know what else to do."

The irony was thick. I was such a hypocrite. I put Sara through the wringer that evening, when I myself—unbeknownst to Sara—had done much worse to her. The night ended with the two of us kissing, our tear-streaked cheeks pressed together, trying to find something that would bring healing and wholeness, trying to find home again.

Feeling Numb

By the end of my senior year, it seemed as if everyone knew what they were doing once they graduated. Many of my classmates were going to graduate school; others had already secured jobs. I, on the other hand, felt numb. I had no idea what to do with an American Studies major. Graduate schools weren't exactly beating down my door to pay me to attend their school, as they were for some of my friends. And I wasn't about to take out student loans to enroll in a graduate program simply for the sake of having something impressive to tell people.

On the other hand, Sara, though not an education major, decided she wanted to teach English at a private school. A few months before graduation she had secured an interview for a teaching position at an exclusive East Coast boarding school. While Sara was perfecting her resume and scouring the Internet for job leads, I sat at my computer and wrote poetry, feeling sorry for myself. I made some halfhearted attempts to find a job, but I had no idea what I was interested in doing. I felt discouraged.

After we graduated, Sara and I knew that we wanted to be together, but it was frightening not knowing what the future held or where Sara's job search might take her. Although Sara had initially been named one of the finalists for the East Coast boarding school position, the school finally decided on the other candidate. Sara was disappointed; I was relieved. To keep her options open, Sara sent her resume to literally hundreds of other schools, and one day, one of those schools called.

California Dream

A Christian school in California unexpectedly called Sara. She was excited, and deservedly so. After only one telephone interview, the school offered to fly her out to California. Sara was thrilled and accepted the offer ("It can't hurt to go out there and interview in person," she said), and the experience did not disappoint. After the interview, the headmaster of the school had Sara stay with his family at their rented beach house for a few days. Sara was in heaven. She not only enjoyed the beach, but she also enjoyed spending time with the headmaster's twenty-two-year-old daughter, who had just graduated from college. By the end of the trip, the California school offered Sara the job—a position teaching high school English.

But there was a conflict. Sara was close to accepting a teaching position in the Midwest. Upon returning from California, Sara debated whether she should accept the job close to home or not. Her heart was in California, but she knew that there was a better chance of us being together if she stayed in the Midwest. So she accepted the job in the Midwest.

But Sara could not get through to anyone in California to let them know she would not be taking the job there. Eventually, through a strange series of coincidences, Sara talked to the headmaster in California, who not only reiterated his desire to have Sara come and teach there, but he also informed Sara that they needed someone for a marketing and public relations position at the school and that, yes, they would be interested in talking to me. Sara was so excited she could hardly contain herself.

After my interview went well with the California school, Sara backed out of the job in the Midwest and took the California job. When they offered me a job as well, I accepted.

The Edge of Myself

When you work for a school, they give you a contract to sign. The day I signed and faxed the contract from my dad's office, I felt as if I were entering the adult world. It was a terrifying feeling. I signed a year of my life on the dotted line and was prepared to pitch my tent with Sara. It was all or nothing now. We would initially live in separate places in California—she would live with a female school administrator, and I with a high school science teacher. But I felt as if marriage were now a certainty, which made me feel even more like an adult.

Sara left two weeks earlier than I did in order to attend a university class. I stayed back in the Midwest, making final preparations to take a leap into the unknown. Saying goodbye to my siblings was the most difficult thing I had to do. I am six and half years older than my brother and eight and a half years older than my sister. I had missed so much of their lives while in college, and now I would miss their high school years as well.

I felt sad.

I was on the edge of myself, looking down, trying to see my future in California, but all I could see was darkness. My future roommate had spent the summer in Canada, and he decided to take a route past my parents' house on his way back to California so that I could follow him out West. I had never been west of Illinois before, so driving across the country was an adventure in and of itself.

As I drove through Utah at dusk—the terrain looking more like Mars than anything else—I realized that I was exhibiting true faith. I had never seen California, let alone where I would work. I was also placing faith in my relationship with Sara. If things didn't end in marriage, I wasn't sure how I would handle it; but if things did end in marriage, I wasn't sure how I would handle that either.

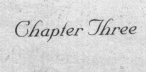

Chapter Three

Engagement

I have run, I have crawled
I have scaled these city walls
Only to be with you
But I still haven't found what I'm looking for
—"I Still Haven't Found What I'm Looking For," U2

Did I really want to marry Sara?

I wasn't sure. We had talked about marriage for nearly two years, but at twenty-two, all I knew was that I didn't want to break up with her. The thought of life without Sara seemed incredibly scary, but the thought of marriage seemed equally so.

Regardless of how I felt, the pressure was on to tie the knot. It was October, and Sara had made it clear that she expected a ring on her finger within the year. "If we're going to have a summer wedding, we had better be engaged by Christmas," she said. "Even then, it's going to be tight getting a wedding planned in that amount of time."

And if she didn't have a ring on her finger soon, then exactly where was our five-year, on-again off-again relationship headed? It was a legitimate question.

I loved Sara, but then again, what did I know about love? Sara was the only real romantic relationship I had ever known. What did I know about marriage? Not much. Sara always talked about marriage as if it would solve all of our problems—as if marriage was some sort of panacea. I never had this impression of married life. I always thought of marriage as something difficult, even for couples who seem to have it all together. And with the emotional highs and lows that our relationship had been through, I didn't consider us to be one of those couples that had it all together. In fact, I wondered if we were ready for marriage at all—or perhaps more accurately, I wondered if I was ready for marriage. Marriage was a huge responsibility and one that I wasn't prepared to enter lightly.

Marriage seemed even more frightening because none of our college friends were married yet. We would be the first ones to marry, and that felt intimidating. Even the thought of proposing to Sara caused my face to burn with embarrassment. I felt everyone would laugh at me behind my back. They would laugh because they knew that I wasn't ready for marriage. Marriage was something adults did, and at twenty-two, I hardly felt like an adult.

One night, I called my parents and told them that I was thinking of asking Sara to marry me. I wanted to gauge their reaction to the news, but it was tough to read between the lines and discern what they really thought. They seemed neither terribly excited nor terribly disappointed. I'm sure that they, like my college friends, expected that it was only a matter of time before I proposed to Sara.

I knew my parents were simply letting me find my own way, but part of me wished they would tell me what to do. I was so desperate for direction of any kind, and they were the ones who I trusted most for such advice. The fact that my parents didn't seem wildly enthusiastic about the possibility of a wedding proposal worried me.

But I was even more worried that I needed outside validation for my decision. Why was I so unsure of myself? As I pondered this question, I finally settled on an answer: I was afraid of commitment. It was true. At twenty-two, I looked young, I thought young, I felt young. There were so many things I wanted to do before I got married—travel, try my hand at different jobs, possibly go back to school for another degree. "But we can do these things together," Sara told me. But I wondered if we ever would do those things.

I remember being so jealous of a friend who was attending graduate school in a Southern California beach town. He seemed to be really living—enjoying himself and pursuing his dreams. My life felt quite different. I felt as if I were only months away from a wife, a mortgage payment, a baby, and a job that didn't seem to fit. This terrified me. I had always dreamed of becoming an actor or a writer, but now that I was faced with the prospect of marriage, my dreams felt as if they would never be realized. My dreams felt incompatible with marriage—at least marriage to Sara.

I considered it a very real possibility that Sara already had our entire lives planned out—what I would do, how many kids we would have, where we would live, who our friends would be, and other details that were known only to her. I worried that I was destined to follow a script that she had already written in her head.

It was tough to know whether I was being selfish, or if God had put certain dreams and desires in my heart for a reason. Sometimes our dreams are whisperings from God; other times, they're selfish desires of our own creation. I used to laugh when I heard people say that they heard this or that from God, but as I look back on my life, I see that God was whispering things to me—things that I ignored. For example, though Sara and I never had sex before we were married, our physical relationship was often more intense than it should've been. I would hear a voice telling me to stop, telling me to respect Sara, telling me to respect myself. And I would disregard that voice.

Once again, I was hearing a voice, this time telling me that I needed to slow down, telling me that I needed to consider whether I was healthy enough to get married. But I closed my ears.

Erwin McManus writes about these whisperings in his book *The Barbarian Way*. At one point he recalls a conversation with his junior high son, Aaron, who wanted to leave summer camp in the middle of the week. Aaron confessed to hearing a voice in his head saying that he should stay and work things out with a boy he had gotten in a fight with. McManus said to him, "Aaron, do you realize what just happened? You heard the voice of the living God. He spoke to you from within your soul. Forget everything else that just happened. God has spoken to you, and you were able to recognize Him."[1]

Looking back on the experience, McManus writes,

> I'll never forget his response: "Well, I'm still not
> doing what He said." I explained to him that
> was his choice, but this is what would happen.
> If he rejected the voice of God and chose to
> disobey His guidance, his heart would become
> hardened, and his ears would become dull. And
> if he continued on this path, there would be a
> day when he would never again hear the voice
> of God. There would come a day when he
> would deny that God even speaks or has ever
> spoken to him. But if he treasured God's voice
> and responded to Him with obedience, then
> his heart would be softened, and his ears would
> always be able to hear the whisper of God into
> his soul.[2]

I wonder if today God seems silent because for so many years I
chose not to listen to Him.

Indecent Proposal

I decided to ask Sara to marry me. I don't remember how I
made my decision. I don't remember waking up one day and
feeling inspired. I don't remember any one moment that solidi-
fied my thinking. Maybe I never considered not marrying Sara,
despite the confusing feelings I had. I guess it came down to
one fact: I couldn't imagine life without her. I wasn't strong
enough to walk away from someone I had cared about for so
long, from someone I had laughed with and cried with, from
someone I loved.

I had followed Sara to California. I had spent hour upon hour
listening to her, talking to her, holding her hand, apologizing,

forgiving, being forgiven. I had put all of my energy into winning her heart. But as I stood on the precipice of marriage, it suddenly seemed like the last thing I wanted.

Still, I had convinced myself it was time to grow up whether I wanted to or not. I had decided that it would be irresponsible to not marry someone I loved, or had loved, or could love again. And so it was under such dubious circumstances that my search for a ring began. One day I made up my mind to go to the mall and begin my quest, all the while dropping hints to Sara that I was going to be out "looking for something special."

As I walked into the jewelry store, I was sure I would say or do something stupid. I remember walking by the glass displays at breakneck speed, my eyes rapidly moving back and forth as my legs carried me forward. I could count on one hand the number of times I had been in a jewelry store before this, and those times were all with my mom or Sara. I had no idea how much an engagement ring would cost, what one should look like, or what kind of ring Sara wanted.

Finally, a woman came up to me and asked if I was looking for anything in particular. My face instantly turned red. I felt beads of sweat forming at my temples as I tried to spit out an answer.

"Well, I'm, ah, I'm looking for an, ah, for an engagement ring."

The woman smiled sympathetically. She had seen dozens if not hundreds of terrified twentysomething guys in her store nervously searching for engagement rings with absolutely no idea what they should be looking for.

She showed me some options in my price range, and I assured

her that I would be back. The entire experience was stressful. I remember returning to my apartment, physically and mentally exhausted. My heart was still beating rapidly as I contemplated whether I was really prepared to make the biggest decision of my life.

I remember asking Sara days later what sort of ring she would like. Her eyes lit up as she described a two-toned ring of white and yellow gold. She even coached me on the various cuts of diamond that were available.

A week later, I was back in the store—this time, slightly more comfortable. I had found a few rings that were strong possibilities. After looking at the choices for twenty minutes, I decided which ring I liked the most and applied for a credit card, which gave me an interest-free, one-year window to pay off the ring. I had never spent so much money on anything in my life. As the jewelry store clerk washed the ring and wrapped it, I began to feel nervous. I was so worried about what I had just done, yet I knew that Sara would be excited, which made me happy. However, I dreaded the phone calls and hysteria that would surely follow my proposal.

It's in the Couch

Though I always thought of myself as romantic, I decided to go ahead with perhaps the lamest wedding proposal of all time. I was afraid of drawing too much attention to the whole thing, so one evening after Sara and I had returned to my apartment to watch television, I managed to sneak the ring box between the cushions of my second-hand couch. I somehow managed to draw Sara's attention to the fact that something was wedged between the cushions, which is when she pulled out the ring box and I got down on one knee.

Sara was excited and incredibly happy, but I could see in her eye that she had a very different sort of wedding proposal in mind. Perhaps she pictured a romantic candlelit dinner at the best restaurant in town, a strolling violinist making his way around the room, as I—dressed in a suit—got down on one knee and read her a poem that I had written for the occasion.

I wonder if the way I proposed was borne out of the fact that I didn't really want to propose in the first place. I wonder if it was borne out of the fact that I felt something more than jitters, something more than doubts. At the time, Sara didn't indicate verbally that she was disappointed with the way I proposed. Yes, she was surprised with how nonchalantly I handled the entire thing, but I think she was so happy to finally have a ring on her finger that any disappointment was quickly replaced by thoughts of invitation lists and bridesmaid dresses.

A few days after I proposed, Sara and I were on a plane home for Christmas. Sara smiled, admiring her ring. She complimented me on my good taste. I, meanwhile, put on my headphones and closed my eyes, terrified by what I had done.

Years later, Sara would recall how I proposed. She would say that I never loved her. She would say that she never loved me. She would say that she wished she never married me.

Chapter Four

Celebrate With Us?

All the promises we make
From the cradle to the grave
When all I want is you

—"All I Want Is You," U2

The wedding plans were moving along quickly, but I was uninvolved and largely uninterested. Sara and her mom talked on the phone daily as they planned the wedding, which was slated for July at a bed and breakfast near Sara's hometown. The location was beautiful. The inn looked like a stone castle, but the wedding would be held outdoors behind the inn, near a river, and the reception in a white tent just a short walk away.

It was stressful for Sara to plan the wedding from so far away. But Sara's mom was an excellent planner and did much of the work. Sara's mom kept a wedding book filled with scraps of paper, magazine pictures, notes, and scribbled phone numbers. Planning the wedding seemed the perfect bonding experience for Sara and her mom; it was something they had dreamed of doing together since Sara was a little girl.

But Sara wanted more than that. She wanted my help, my involvement, and, perhaps most of all, my interest. I think she resented the fact that I had so little to do with the wedding.

However, even if I had been interested in helping plan the wedding, I'm not sure how much input I would've had. Some time before the wedding, Sara handed me a catalog with pictures of tuxedos. She told me to pick out the one that I liked the most, the one that I would wear as we became husband and wife. I came back with my suggested tuxedo, but Sara said it wasn't formal enough. So we went with a more formal tuxedo, one that Sara preferred. It was a minor squabble, but I was bothered by the fact that I wouldn't even have control over what I would wear for the biggest day of my life.

In fact, as I look back, I realize that everything I did for the wedding was something already planned for me—like the wedding shower. As Sara smiled graciously and opened the gifts, I sat in a chair next to her, trying not to blush. Sitting in a room full of women, I imagined everyone thinking, "They're so young." I felt like my mom's eyes were boring into the side of my head as she wondered if I really knew what I was doing.

The marriage plans rolled onward, as unstoppable as ocean waves. The wedding seemed to take on a life of its own. It was a force of nature, pushing me out into the water, deeper and deeper. It would eventually wear away the good and bad parts of me, just as water shapes a rock cliff.

Wedding Assignments

About five months before the wedding, Sara began telling me that we should talk to our pastor in California about premarital counseling. Premarital counseling was very popular in the evangelical circles that I came from, and our pastor in California had counseled scores of couples before their weddings.

Sara encouraged me for weeks to talk to our pastor about this, but I put it off. That is until one Sunday when I found myself sheepishly walking up to the pastor after his sermon, asking him if he did premarital counseling in a sort of "aw shucks" way. I knew that it would be a good thing to do, yet I didn't want to do it. It felt like too much work. Looking back, I wonder if I didn't want to do it for one reason in particular: I was afraid of what I might discover about myself, about Sara, about us. I may have been worried that I would realize we had many deep unresolved problems—things that should've forced us to reconsider marriage in the first place. The whole purpose of premarital counseling was to actually see if you were right for one another, but Sara and I had already made up our minds: We were getting married. The counseling was a mere formality.

On the first day of counseling, we were given a workbook filled with assignments to complete before each meeting. The book had Bible verses about men and women and marriage littered throughout, verses you had to look up and answer questions about. Much of the book focused on the roles of the husband and wife—it kept saying that I, as the husband, had to be the leader, but I didn't feel like the leader. I felt like a piece of driftwood floating out into the dark water.

I remember going to a park with Sara to work on the book together, but I kept talking about other things. I kept telling jokes, and Sara was getting frustrated. "Are we going to work on this or not?" she asked. "I feel like you're not taking this seriously."

She was right. I wasn't.

The Sex Talk

Weeks later, the pastor talked to us about sex. I remember the uneasy feeling I had as the pastor looked at us from his chair, carefully explaining how sex can be painful for a woman, especially the first few times. To say the moment was awkward is an understatement.

For me sex was the "payoff" for getting married. Sara and I were both virgins when we married. I imagined what our first night together would be like, how wonderful it would be. But I have to admit that I was terrified of sex. More specifically, I was terrified of being pathetically bad at it.

Sex was often on my mind those days. I began looking at Internet pornography. Late at night I would turn on the computer and click on images of naked women. One was never enough. Afterward, I would go to bed—defeated, feeling like hell, praying that I would never do it again. But, of course, I would, in large part because no one knew. Looking at Internet pornography seemed like something you should never tell anyone, which is probably why it has become a hidden epidemic.

Sara never knew I was looking at pornography, and if she had, she would have been horrified. Lust and pornography are substitutes for genuine relationships, which might have explained my sudden attraction to these images. In many ways, Sara and I didn't have a genuine relationship: I refused to share deeply and honestly with her, and she refused to listen to deep and honest thoughts that she might not agree with.

Making Preparations

Because we both worked for a school, Sara and I had most of the summer off. I had to work two weeks longer than she did, but Sara needed to get home to finalize wedding plans. As I dropped Sara off in Los Angeles for her flight, tears rolled down my cheeks. Despite our problems, I loved Sara and didn't want her to leave.

After she left, I secured an apartment across the street from where we both worked. We would be sharing a car during our first year of marriage, and the location of the apartment couldn't have been more convenient.

We began paying for the apartment in June, which not only eliminated the worry of having to find a place when we returned in August, but it also gave us somewhere to store our things for the summer. My last few nights in California were spent in that apartment on a second-hand couch, surrounded by piles of clothes and boxes. I remember talking to Sara on the phone, explaining the layout and what floor it was located on, hoping that I had picked one she would like.

A few days after I had temporarily set up camp in the new apartment, I left California for a work-related conference in Austin, Texas. After the conference, the plan was to continue driving home to the Midwest, where I'd spend about a week at my parents' house before the wedding.

One of my last nights in Austin, I stood on a beautiful deck overlooking a lake, talking to a fellow attendee who I knew from the school in California. A successful businessman, he was also a school board member. I told him about my impending wedding, and he said, "Getting married is the best thing that I ever did. You're going to love it."

For maybe the first time ever, I felt peace about my decision to get married. Eric was a man of integrity—the sort of person no one would ever say anything bad about, and he was saying, "Cameron, getting married is great." For once, I thought, "Maybe he's right. Maybe this will be the best thing that's ever happened to me."

Here Comes the Bride

I stood inside the inn with my tux on, waiting for the cue to walk outside and stand in front of two hundred people. My best man stood next to me, hand on my shoulder, and prayed. I don't know what he prayed, but it felt good to be quiet and breathe deeply as he spoke. I had always thought it silly when people talked about being nervous before weddings. I thought, "What's there to be nervous about? You stand there, and it's over." But now I knew what they meant. In a few minutes, my life would change forever.

The thought of being naked in front of Sara created a desire to run and do sit-ups and any sort of physical exercise I could think of, not because I was in bad shape, but because I wanted to look stronger and healthier and better than I did. I wanted Sara to be attracted to me. I also wanted Sara to be happy and fulfilled.

As terrified as I was about getting married—as many questions as I still had—I really did love Sara. I knew that I could be a good husband if I worked at becoming one. I also knew that I was immature and needed to grow up. I kept telling myself that marriage would do the trick in a hurry, and in many ways, it did.

I was almost shaking as I walked out and took my place in front of the assembled crowd. The day was slightly overcast but warm. Earlier in the morning it had been beautiful, but the sky threatened rain as the afternoon wore on. I stood in the late afternoon warmth, the river behind me, and in front of me, plastic chairs, well-dressed people, and tall, stately trees hovering over the makeshift outdoor chapel. I watched with some trepidation as the music began and the groomsmen escorted the bridal party to their positions. My sister was in the bridal party, and my brother was a groomsman. Sara's sister was also in the bridal party, and her two brothers were groomsmen. I also had two of my closest friends as groomsmen, and my best friend from college was the best man.

Then the string quartet started playing that song—the one I'd heard hundreds of times on television and in movies—and Sara entered. She looked beautiful. She was dressed in white, with elaborate stitching on her gown, her light brown hair in rolls of tight braids behind an elegant veil. She was truly the perfect bride. Yet I felt almost emotionless. I kept thinking about how I should be smiling or crying or something as she walked down the aisle with her father. I knew that people were watching, so I forced a smile as I stood there, stiff as starch in my black tuxedo.

As Sara's dad handed over his daughter, a tear began to form, and his voice quivered as he answered, "Her mother and I do," to the question, "Who gives this woman in holy matrimony?" He sat down in the front row and wiped his eyes. While the pastor spoke, a jackhammer from somewhere nearby made a loud thundering noise that echoed across the river. No one objected to the marriage, but the jackhammer continued to roar over the pastor's voice. The pastor gave an abbreviated sermon, and I stood there blankly. When we finally exchanged the vows, I still felt nervous but almost happy. Sara looked so beautiful. I knew that I was lucky to have someone who was so smart and kind and attractive.

But why wasn't I happier? If this was the best day of my life, why didn't I feel like it? As Sara and I walked down the aisle after the ceremony, people clapped. We stood on the stately lawn and waited to receive our guests. Our parents joined us at our sides, with my mom arriving first and looking at my ring with a mix of joy and trepidation. She was almost crying as she said something that betrayed her surprise that I actually did it, that I was actually married.

The Rain

It started raining soon after the reception began, but the guests were dry under the large, white tent. Almost as soon as it started raining, it stopped again. When it stopped, my dad pulled me aside and pointed to the sky, where there was a rainbow.

"Cam, look. That's God's provision for you. It's His blessing on this day."

It is a moment that I will forever remember, because as wonderful as my dad's thought was, it simply wasn't true—at least not entirely true.

It might have been God's provision, but it wasn't His blessing. Not on this marriage, not on this day, not on this wedding. It rained again that day, as hours later drops of rainwater fell from the sides of the tent. Inside, people danced on dry ground and drank wine and took pictures and laughed. I didn't know it then, but it would rain throughout my marriage. And when it stopped raining, there would be no chirping birds or brilliant rainbows. There would be only emptiness and dark clouds and the threat of more rain.

The First Night

After the wedding and reception, Sara and I went up to our room in the inn. The room had wooden floors, a fireplace, and a king-sized bed. It was decorated in a beautiful combination of old and new, antique and modern.

It was midnight, and Sara and I were exhausted. Yet as we opened the door to our room, we both were infused with a strange sort of energy. This was it—our night to stand in front of each other naked and unashamed.

As Sara showered, I sat in a small foyer attached to our bedroom and watched *SportsCenter*. I tried to calm myself as I watched the sports highlights, which on this night were completely uninteresting to me. I was nervous and excited and terrified about what would transpire when Sara left the bathroom. Soon I turned off the television and walked into the other room. Not knowing what else to do, I sat on the bed, waiting for Sara as patiently as I could. After ten minutes on the bed, I started to wonder if she would ever come out of the bathroom.

But as soon as I started to give up hope, the door opened, and there she was. I was stunned. I had never seen anyone so beautiful. I stood up and walked over to her, and we embraced and kissed. "You look so beautiful," I said. Sara smiled.

As we kissed and fell on the bed, I in my youth and foolishness quickly started to move toward my goal: sex. It never occurred to me that women were different than men when it came to sex, that it took time for them to get comfortable and feel excited. And our first sexual foray was painful for Sara and humiliating for me. In fact, it couldn't have gone much worse. When Sara and I went to sleep that night, we didn't feel like one soul.

We instead felt angry and frustrated and ashamed. And all my insecurities about sex rose to the surface.

I began to think that, indeed, I would never be good at sex and that Sara and I would never have a fulfilling sexual relationship. I immediately began to associate sex with failure. The evening did not go as Sara had imagined it either, and she was visibly frustrated. I sighed and stared at the ceiling as she fell asleep.

The Honeymoon

Sara and I left the next day for Jamaica. We stayed at an all-inclusive resort, and the grounds were beautiful. Lush palm trees, exotic flowers, and wild gardens were only steps from a private beach that hugged warm, crystal clear water.

Arriving at the hotel, I could feel the tropical air blowing lightly across marble floors and desktops. A Jamaican employee sat down with us, explaining where our room was, what services the hotel offered, and what restaurants were on the property. He also handed us warm washcloths and glasses of champagne.

The scene could not have been more romantic, but frustration and disappointment were palpable, a foreshadowing of more awkward moments in the bedroom, more arguments. It seemed strange that I could feel so uneasy and frustrated during the one time that was supposed to be so idyllic in our married lives.

Things came to a head one day when, as we walked to the pool, Sara accused me of looking at another woman in a bathing suit. I denied it, but she was right: I was looking at someone else. What was wrong with me? How could I be so ugly, so sinful to be looking at other women when I was with the woman I had just promised to love and cherish forever? Perhaps it was sexual frustration, but that seems a lame excuse for a deeper problem that I had—a problem with lust.

Family Vacation

Returning from our honeymoon, Sara and I had one more trip to take before we drove back to California. Each summer, my parents, siblings, uncles, aunts, and cousins took a weeklong vacation to a resort in the Midwest. Sara and I had been invited to join them, which we did as soon as we returned from Jamaica.

It was odd suddenly going from a kid in the eyes of my family to a twenty-three-year-old husband, and I think it was a difficult transition for my parents as well. I was the oldest of three, and this was their first experience as in-laws.

Sara felt that as soon as we got to the resort, my mom wanted us to spend all of our time with her—which, of course, made Sara want to spend all of our time away from my mom. Sara could feel my mom hovering, listening to our every word, trying to insert herself into all of our conversations.

To some extent, Sara's observations were correct. I think my mom worried that somehow getting married meant that I would gradually disassociate myself from the family until I no longer spent any time with them at all. Perhaps this was because she could feel the tension in her relationship with Sara. I'm sure my mom also sensed that Sara could be controlling and that she would pull me away from the family if she ever got tired of them.

Maybe my mom was clinging to the past as a result, clinging to the way life was before I was married. Perhaps she was trying to convince herself that things wouldn't change—didn't have to change. But they had changed and, in fact, needed to change due to the very fact that Sara was now the most important person in my life.

When Sara would say things about my mom—how this or that was irritating—I would let her vent and then sweep it under the rug and hope it went away. But it didn't go away.

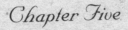

Chapter Five

All That You Can't Leave Behind

**It's a long way down
to nothing at all**

—"Stuck in a Moment ...," U2

With a cartop carrier full of luggage and wedding gifts packed like *Tetris* blocks in the back seat, Sara and I set out for California. Michigan was a blur as we left in rain drops, but we found the sun in Indiana and followed it through Illinois.

Our trip would take us through several states, including the corn fields of Iowa, the open plains of Nebraska, and the mountains of Colorado and Utah. The scenery moved from ugly to majestic to strangely beautiful to ugly again. Such is the pattern of life, and my relationship with Sara was no exception. But as we drove across the country—road maps spilling onto the floor—I had trouble pinpointing exactly where I was on the emotional landscape.

In between green forests and brown California deserts, I tried to make sense of the living and the dying and the marrying. I began to reflect on the road thus far as Sara slept in the seat next to me, the drone of the car's wheels making me, too, crave sleep. I thought of tears—tears that fell when Sara left college one summer without a goodbye, tears that fell when Sara needed a break from "us." But I also thought of happiness—happiness I felt when Sara returned from Europe, happiness I felt as Sara and I walked across San Diego beaches.

And now here I was, my life streaming by through windows, green rows of corn marching step for step with the car. How did I feel now? I felt uneasy. There was so much to learn, so much to sacrifice. And still the question that hung over me like a shroud: Would I be happy? I didn't know. Everyone told me that I would be, but I had my doubts. The funny thing was that even if I wasn't happy, I knew that would be okay. Marriage wasn't about being happy, right? In fact, I wondered if happiness was a paradox. I wondered if happiness was only found in making someone else happy.

And Miles to Go Before We Sleep

As miles wore down and days passed, Sara and I played a game. We would tell each other as much as we could about the state we were driving through. Sara would talk about someone she knew from each state, while I would list the area's major cities, sports teams, and universities. We would laugh, enjoying each other, enjoying silly conversation, enjoying the fact that we were completely ourselves and no longer worried about impressing one another.

Snapshots flash through my mind from our cross-country trip: Sara and I at a Mexican restaurant in Iowa City with me sporting a sparsely grown goatee and Sara wearing a red-and-white bandanna; Sara and I posing in front of a scenic outlook in Utah, desolate, conical hills behind us. I am wearing Sara's sunglasses in the waning sunlight as a Japanese tourist takes our picture.

The trip was fun, but bed called as we rolled into hotel parking lots at dusk. And each night as we prepared for bed, I felt a pain in my chest. Our failure to have satisfying sex weighed heavily on me, and I could feel myself withdrawing from Sara despite the strong sexual feelings that I had for her. I was so scared at the thought of trying and failing to satisfy her, and I think that she too began to withdraw from physical contact. The topic became one that we discussed less and less. We hardly knew how to approach something that suddenly seemed so sensitive and intensely personal.

The pressure and disappointment and frustration continued to build as we entered California and drove through mountain passes and into the desert. The hills became pale and the air hot with the late afternoon sun. We passed the windmills that we knew so well, and suddenly everything felt quiet, including my heart. The area where we lived was a strangely beautiful place with misshapen trees, hard-shelled animals, and lonely sandcastle mountains.

As we pulled into our apartment complex, I was reminded of the look and texture of so many of the desert homes and buildings: a sort of earthy siding that conjures up images of the red clay used to make adobe dwellings. We parked the car and walked up to the apartment—a long outdoor staircase leading up to the second floor. I opened the door.

Sara was happy with the apartment, especially with the large bathroom—until we opened the plastic shower door. Because the apartment was so warm (and had been vacant for nearly a month), the door shattered as soon as we slid it open. There were sharp pieces of plastic everywhere. Twenty minutes later, Sara laughed and snapped a picture of me in my underwear sweeping shards of plastic into a dustpan. "Burn that picture," I said, smirking. Sara laughed mischievously. And as she laughed, I suddenly felt that things would work out, that things would be okay. Why wouldn't they be okay? We loved each other.

But as I lay in bed that night, my eyes refused to shut. I knew something was wrong, but I brushed it off, convincing myself that I was only nervous about being married. Yet I wondered why being married to Sara felt so disquieting.

I Love My Job, I Hate Mine

Sara was an amazing teacher, and she loved what she was doing. She was often perplexed as to why it took her four years of college to realize that she wanted to be a teacher, yet it should have been clear that her entire life had been preparing her for the job. Sara's role model was her mom, and her mom was the ultimate teacher. For Sara's mom, every moment was a "teachable" moment. She would review Sara's homework at night and create tests and assignments for her to complete. She even required daily reading times throughout the summer.

Sara had always loved school, perhaps because she always did so well. She had mastered the art of studying, and by the time college rolled around, Sara was almost a professional when it came to studying. She knew exactly what to study, when to study it, and for how long. She imparted the same wisdom to her students. She also had a strong desire to nurture, love, and support the kids whom she taught.

Sara managed to achieve a balance that few teachers ever attain—her students respected her in the classroom but found her approachable outside of it. Students were always in Sara's classroom—before school, after school. Whenever Sara was there, she was certain to have a student nearby, talking to her. Sara's youth—and she looked even younger than she was—seemed a source of constant fascination for the high school students. They loved asking her questions about anything—the decorations on her desk, why her room was so clean, what state she was from, what she liked about California, how many siblings she had—virtually anything interested her students.

I, on the other hand, hadn't found my dream job. I did a little bit of this, a little bit of that—fundraising, marketing, public relations, taught a class here and there. I felt as if I were there simply because the school wanted Sara so badly. I was also impatient with the idea of paying my dues in the working world, especially because I quickly knew that working for a school wasn't my niche. Despite the fact that I was surrounded by wonderful people, my days were an exercise in frustration. I pictured myself doing something more exciting than writing school newsletters.

It didn't help that I often thought of my friends and what they were doing. Two were in law school, another was getting his PhD, another was getting a master's at one of the most beautiful universities in the country, and one was in seminary. My friends' lives seemed so much more exciting than mine. Of course, the grass always seems greener on the other side.

"I just feel like I'm not doing what I'm supposed to be doing," I would complain to Sara.

"Well, what do you want to do?" she would ask.

"I don't know. But not this."

Life as We Knew It

Marriage was not all that Sara and I thought it would be. It was difficult. In addition to the sexual frustration that we both felt, there were other problems, such as figuring out how to handle all of the day-to-day things that come with living with another person, things such as cleaning and cooking and listening and managing relationships with friends and in-laws. In-laws were the biggest problem. As Sara's frustration with my mom grew, I became increasingly confused about how to handle it—or even what the problem was.

"What is she saying to you?" I asked Sara.

"It's not always what she says—it's how she says it," Sara replied.

I ignored her concerns for months until finally they couldn't be ignored any longer. Sara began rolling her eyes whenever my parents would call. She would worry for weeks before seeing them, once having to go to the doctor because the stress was physically making her sick. "We need to talk to someone about this," she finally said one day. "I can't stand this any longer."

"Sara, what are you talking about? I don't understand why we need to talk to someone about this. I really don't want to see anyone," I said.

I began taking my parents' side, thinking that it was all in Sara's head, thinking that Sara was paranoid. Not surprisingly, Sara began to resent this. I tried to see Sara's side, tried to convince myself that my mom was being difficult, but anytime I told Sara that her concerns were valid, I was lying. I just didn't see what was so bothersome.

Moving Home

After a year as a married couple in California, things were close to hitting rock bottom. Sara was tired of me complaining about my job. She also felt betrayed by some of her students who had recently been caught with drugs. She was stressed out and had almost had it—with me, with school, with life.

As we considered whether or not to sign a new contract for the upcoming school year, we began talking about moving. Did we want to stay in California? If not, where would we go? Where would we work? We weren't sure. However, things were coming to a head with Sara and my parents. She had been pressuring me to go to counseling with her, and I continually refused, saying that she was exaggerating, saying that there was nothing happening with my parents that required counseling.

Sara didn't like my answer, and she said that if we moved back to the Midwest, she would not let us move anywhere near my mom. As the deadline to sign a new contract grew nearer, the pressure mounted to make a decision. I called my dad one day and laid out all of the positives and negatives for staying, and then I asked him what I should do. "Son, I can't tell you what to do. You need to make that decision," he said. That was wise advice, but I simply wanted someone to tell me what I should do, what we should do. Sara made it clear that she was putting the decision in my lap. "You're the one who doesn't like working here ... you're the one who doesn't like California," she said.

"Sara, I like California. I just feel like my job isn't a good fit ... I feel like I'm not doing what I'm supposed to be doing."

"You don't like California. You've never liked California," Sara said. "Why don't we just move? That's what you want to do."

"Well, what do you want to do? What do you think we should do?" I asked.

"I don't care, but you're the leader, and you need to make that decision. And as the leader, you will be held responsible for whatever decision you make, good or bad," Sara said. "You will be judged before God."

Sara's words were almost apocalyptic.

"Before God ... Judged ... You."

Her words were filled with fire and brimstone. In the circles we ran in, we were always told that the husband was the unquestioned leader—the Bible said so. But didn't the Bible also teach mutual submission? Didn't the Bible teach that both husband and wife were equal in the marriage and in any relationship? Sara didn't think so, and the pressure for me to make all the decisions—and all the right ones—sometimes felt overwhelming. Especially when I was asked to make decisions that would drastically affect our lives, such as moving across the country.

I wrote out the pros and cons of moving and picked Sara's brain as I created the list. The results were inconclusive, so I finally said, "Let's move." Those two words produced a flurry of activity. We told the school administrators we were leaving. We picked the city in the Midwest where we would move, one that was close—but not too close—to both of our families. We began searching for jobs. And a few weeks later, in the middle of the summer before either of us had even secured employment, we moved. Sara's mom found an apartment for us to live in—one that we had only seen on the Internet. A moving company came and packed up the furniture that we had bought earlier that year, and Sara and I packed many of the other items we had. And again, for the second time in a year, we packed our car and moved back across the country.

But as we prepared to leave, I realized that Sara and I could never truly run away from our past, from ourselves, from our problems. We had to face them, and it would be ugly.

The Trip Back

The car trip across the country was equal parts silence and serious conversation. Sara and I had come to a crux in our relationship and were finally forced to broach serious topics. In the car, I gave Sara my undivided attention and started listening to her concerns about my mom. I finally started to acknowledge that we had problems. I even admitted that maybe we needed to talk to someone—maybe even a marriage counselor.

We talked about how the two of us expressed love, how we differed in what we needed from one another to feel loved. While these sorts of conversations were desperately needed, they opened up other areas of concern, other areas of pain.

By facing the truth, I was suddenly aware that healthy relationships didn't happen by accident. Healthy relationships were a lot of work, though perhaps not as much for those whose personalities complemented one another. Together, Sara and I were a volatile pair. Our backgrounds and temperaments were constantly in conflict. We were both first-borns, which is maybe one reason why we frequently locked horns. Sara was also a controller, and I resented being controlled. But I was never strong enough to speak up about my concerns, or maybe I didn't even understand them. As we arrived at our new apartment in an unfamiliar city, all we had was each other—and God.

God never factored into our relationship enough. We never seemed to move past our own selfishness to see something—someone—bigger than ourselves. We should have been stuck together with God's glue, as the U2 song "Staring at the Sun" says, but we were only stuck together by a marriage certificate and rings on our left hands. God was never the foundation of our relationship. He was only a nice add-on that we sometimes took off the shelf when it seemed convenient or needed.

Our first night in our new apartment was awful. Sara was crying, saying that I hadn't made her my top priority, that I always sided with my parents. I prayed that God would help, that God would show me what to do. I told Sara that we could go see a counselor because I cared about her and our marriage, but she was still sad and worried. She told me that I never seemed sad or worried enough. Unconvincingly, I assured her that I was.

In fact, I was worried, too. I just didn't trust Sara with my feelings, so she rarely saw them. It had been a long time since I had trusted her with my feelings. I think I stopped when she was telling me how I should feel when we first moved to California, when she started telling me that it was immature to miss my friends and family, that it was immature to need anyone other than her. "Why am I not enough?" she would ask.

I learned to bury my feelings in search of the "right" feelings. I would bury them and hope that they would go away. But they never did. They would stay submerged for a time, but they always floated back to the surface. But I was an actor by training, so I could usually project calmness even when all I felt was chaos inside.

That evening as Sara sat on the floor and cried, I wondered whether we would ever leave behind the pain, the past, and the frustration.

Help Us

A pastor gave us the name of a marriage counselor. I remember the nervousness I felt during our first session as we met in his office one spring afternoon. Sara had recently taken a job at a publishing house, and she left work early and met me there. I had no problem making the appointment. I had been working as a freelance writer, and the work was sparse at first, which concerned Sara. After we met in the parking lot, we silently took the long walk up the stairs to the second-story suite in an inconspicuous office building.

After signing in and waiting for ten minutes, we were called into the counselor's office. He was a tall, distinguished-looking man in his mid- to late-fifties with glasses, a closely cropped beard, and wavy brown hair. After some chitchat, coffee, and firm handshakes, the counselor got down to business.

"What do you want to get out of counseling," he asked, his fingers interlocked as he sat back in his leather chair. I nervously fidgeted with an empty Styrofoam coffee cup that he had handed me minutes earlier, and as I did so, I realized that Sara was staring at me, waiting for me to answer the question.

"Well ... we're here because of some problems that we have ... mainly with my parents," I stammered as I ripped off an edge of the cup. "We, ah, well ... it's been a tough marriage, and I guess this has been the biggest issue ... mainly how Sara feels that my mom has treated her unfairly and how I haven't really done much to help make things better ... I guess, how I've actually not taken Sara's side and ... well, that's really hurt her feelings."

Sara interjected, "Cameron is supposed to protect me as his wife, and as the leader, he hasn't done a good job of that. He always takes his parents' side and never wants to see how much they hurt me. I was actually getting physically sick in California because I was so stressed out about this, and Cameron literally did nothing."

The counselor sat and listened, his shoulders slung back and his head low, eyes peering over his glasses. Throughout the session he nodded, occasionally scribbling notes on a legal pad.

As we left that day, neither Sara nor I felt better, but we knew we had done the right thing by talking to a counselor.

Ironically, I was more optimistic than Sara was about counseling. Despite Sara's pessimism about whether things would ever get better, we returned to the counseling office every two weeks. We ended up talking about many things, including the unhealthy way that we settled arguments, which usually involved me burying my feelings and Sara trying to exert control over me. But the main topic of discussion was my parents. It was an issue that Sara felt had to be solved. She was going to either explode or simply refuse to ever talk to my mom again.

After several sessions, the counselor suggested that we meet with my parents. The idea was that I would moderate the meeting and keep it civil. After a week or two, I finally agreed, though I admitted it made me nervous.

A Meeting with the Parents

I told my parents that I wanted to meet with them and discuss something. They were surprised but receptive to the idea.

"What do you want to talk about?" my mom asked.

"Well, I just think there are some things we should discuss—I don't want to get into it on the phone, but I think we'll all feel better once we talk," I said.

Walking into my parents' house that afternoon, I felt my stomach tightening. I'd rehearsed in my head what I would say, and I held Sara's hand as we walked into the living room and sat down—Sara and I next to each other in chairs, my mom on the couch, and my dad in a chair next to her.

"Well, I'm glad we could all meet today," I said, my voice louder than I had expected and my words surprisingly formal. "I think before we get started there are a few things I should say. Um, well … first of all, Sara and I have had a tough marriage. And, well, so far one of our big struggles has been how to handle our relationship with the two of you."

My mom looked at me quizzically. It was as if she were silently asking who put me up to this.

"Sara and I have actually been meeting with a marriage counselor—that's how big of a deal this has become—and Sara was getting physically sick in California because she was so stressed about her relationship with the two of you," I said.

"Oh, my goodness," my dad said.

His eyes narrowed. He looked at me intently.

"Well, I haven't done a very good job of listening to Sara's concerns, but I think I've learned a lot these past few months. And, uh, well, one of the things that we talked about with the counselor was how maybe I've had trouble grasping the idea that things are different now that I'm married, the idea that Sara has to be my first priority."

It was tough for me to confront my parents with things that were causing problems in my marriage.

"I think that maybe the two of you have had difficulty with me being married too, which is probably natural since I'm the old-est and you've never had to deal with any of us being married before," I said. "So I guess I just wanted to talk about all of that and give Sara a chance to say what she's thinking, too ... but I definitely want it all to be done in a healthy way ... I don't want anyone to get too upset. I don't want any of us to be disrespect-ful toward each other."

I felt as if I were having an out-of-body experience. Sitting there having a discussion that I didn't want to have with Sara, whose anger I didn't fully understand; sitting there having a discussion with my parents, who I had never confronted with something as serious as this. I was in an awkward position. But they were my parents and I was Sara's husband, and so I tried to act more mature than I felt; I tried to become something I wasn't; I tried to will myself to have control of the situation.

"I had no idea that this was a problem," my mom said.

I could feel Sara getting angry. She had predicted that my mom would play dumb.

"She's passive-aggressive," Sara had told me days earlier. "She'll make herself look like the victim."

"Mom, I wonder if maybe you were upset when I followed Sara to California. Do you think that you were upset and then un-intentionally took it out on Sara?" I asked. I was parroting back things that Sara had said, things that the counselor had asked about. But this was a point that I actually thought had some validity. I thought that maybe my mom did feel put-off by the fact that I left for California, and that as I grew closer to Sara, I became increasingly isolated from her.

"No ... no ... gosh, I wasn't angry when you left," my mom said. "I really don't think so at all."

"But you always say things," Sara said. "When you ask questions, they're always asked in a negative way: 'Teaching's a lot of work, isn't it? It's really hard, isn't it?' And I'll say, 'Yeah, it is a lot of work, but I love it.' It's as if I'm always on the defensive."

Sara continued. Her voice was strained. "You're always doubting me ... it's so frustrating."

"I don't feel that I've ever done that, Sara ... I'm trying to think about it now, and I don't feel that I've done that ... not inten-tionally," my mom said.

"But I think you have," Sara said strongly. "You have done it intentionally. I don't know how you couldn't have." Sara was raising her voice, which made my mom, who is naturally quiet, uncomfortable.

Sara continued to get agitated, as more than a year of frustration suddenly bubbled to the surface. And then my mom started to raise her voice.

"Okay, let's make sure that everyone is talking about how they feel ... let's make sure we word things so that this can be productive," I said.

A few minutes later, things had calmed down, and it seemed a natural time to wrap up the conversation.

"Well, at least everyone expressed their concerns. I know that we probably didn't solve everything, but I guess it was good just to talk about it," I said.

Sara actually did look better, calmer, and she stood up and talked to my mom before we left. They both hugged, and my mom started to cry and apologized to Sara for any misunderstanding.

"I wish we would've known," my dad said as Sara and my mom embraced. "We could have talked about this a long time ago."

Despite some tense moments, things suddenly seemed as if they might be okay. Sara squeezed my hand as we pulled away from my parents' house. "You did a good job," she said. "I'm still bothered by some things, but I do feel a lot better."

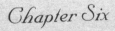

Chapter Six

A Bad Moment

In the garden I was playing the tart
I kissed your lips and broke your heart
You were acting like it was the end of the world

—"Until the End of the World," U2

One Saturday evening, Sara and I stood at the counter of a
bookstore café ordering coffee when something happened:
A magazine caught my eye. It was an issue of *Maxim*, a men's
magazine filled with photos of half-naked women. From the
chrome counter, a beautiful, big-breasted brunette in a bathing
suit stared up at me. I looked once, twice, three times, maybe
four. Sara noticed. And when she did, I instantly knew that
something dreadful was about to happen, or more precisely had
already happened.

"Did you look at that magazine?" she asked as we sat down with our cups of coffee.

"What magazine?"

Sara was disgusted. "Did you look at that magazine or not?" she asked again, this time her blue eyes turning to pots of boiling water.

I was terrified of her—perhaps because I had created for her a persona that I could never equal, a persona that I would forever chase but never catch. I was the second coming of Jesus, or so I had convinced Sara. In reality, I resembled the devil much more than I did Jesus. I was constantly hiding my true self out of fear. I found trite, dishonest conversation much easier than raw, truthful conversation. "Yeah, that sounds good. I like your suggestion. Let's do that," I would often say in order to avoid disagreement.

I also lied to uphold my reputation as a good Christian. It seemed that Sara always needed me to be better than I was. She needed to feel that I was above moral reproach, and I never wanted to disappoint her. It was a standard she never held her father or brothers to—she could easily overlook a crass comment from one of them—though she certainly assumed that they, too, were above the sins of lust and dishonesty. Of course, they weren't. Who among us is?

Sara once told me about a conversation she had with a friend whose boyfriend readily admitted a fondness for paging through Victoria's Secret catalogs. Sara's friend said, "I'm sure Cameron and his friends do the same thing. Most guys do." Sara was offended and assured her friend with no small degree of indignation that I didn't. "Cameron would never look through a Victoria's Secret catalog; that's ridiculous."

Of course, she was wrong, and her friend was right. But I nodded reassuringly as Sara recounted the conversation, saying, "Yes, you're right. I would never do such a thing."

No woman wants to believe that her husband or boyfriend is easily trapped by lust, but both common sense and professional research confirm the ugly truth that men are easily lured away from sexual purity. It hurts. It makes women feel undesirable; it cheapens relationships ... not to mention it offends God.

But for Sara, the sin of lust was more than a universal human experience—something that makes us all sinful, something that leaves all of us in need of grace from God and each other. For Sara, it was a sin that stood high above the rest, a sin that she seemed to be obsessed with. It makes me wonder if her experience within the evangelical subculture made her more sensitive to lust. Perhaps disingenuous Christians like me had somehow convinced her that faith was a destination and not a journey— that once you "became" a Christian, you suddenly and magically abandoned all of the ugly baggage that you brought with you. Of course, this isn't true. After all, wasn't it the apostle Paul who wrote, "The very thing I do not want to do, I do"? Or was Sara's sensitivity to lust the result of something entirely different? Perhaps Sara reacted so strongly because of something from her past, something she experienced in another relationship, or maybe something she saw as a child.

That evening in the bookstore café, none of these thoughts came to mind. I was only concerned about survival: the survival of my marriage. Something told me that my answer to the question "Did you look at that magazine?" held implications far beyond what I could fathom. So I resorted to my favorite survival mechanism: I lied.

"The magazine on the counter? No, I didn't look at that magazine—why? Why are you asking me this?"

My heart raced; my hands felt cold and clammy. Sara said nothing. She knew I was lying.

"Sara, why are you asking me this?"

"I saw you look at it," she said, her eyes locked on mine, her face frozen.

"Yeah, I guess I did. I guess I did look at it. I'm sorry," I said, looking down at my hands.

After a few moments of silence, we instinctively stood up, walked to the car, and drove home. More silence. The streets were dark, the passing cars noiseless. My heart thundered in my chest. A seven-minute drive back to our apartment felt as if it would never end.

When we arrived home, Sara began firing questions at me. Each question was asked with more desperation than the one before. I began pacing, taking shallow breaths. My chest felt heavy. Sara sat upright on the couch—every muscle in her body taut, as if she were preparing for fight or flight, the two adrenaline-fueled responses of humans and animals. Her face looked contorted— she pulled her mouth to the side and narrowed her eyes.

"Tell me what else you've done. Tell me how often you look at magazines like this," she said. "I know you're not just looking at these things—you're acting out, you're masturbating, aren't you? I knew you were a liar ... you've been lying to me all along, haven't you? So what else have you done? What else don't I know about? You're looking at other women, aren't you?"

"No," I said. "What are you talking about? Just because I looked at that magazine, you're asking all of these things? Sara, this is crazy. This is just crazy."

But she wouldn't stop. "You're lying. I know you're lying."

She kept pushing and pushing. I grew exhausted and fidgety as it approached midnight. I kept rubbing my eyes, scratching my head, grabbing the back of my neck with my right hand, absent-mindedly massaging it. I felt as if Sara were a detective trying to produce a confession. As she continued to lob accusations at me, my resistance weakened. Her tactic worked surprisingly well because I finally admitted something, but only enough to get her to stop asking questions—or so I thought.

"Yes, I guess I have struggled with this before—with looking at other women or glancing at magazines—not pornography but magazines like the one in the bookstore."

But she fired back with more questions—anger and questions.

"Yes, I have masturbated before. I have struggled with that, but not very often."

I lied. The truth is, like most guys, I had struggled with masturbation repeatedly, and before we were married, I had also struggled with Internet pornography for a time. But as I saw

Sara's anger, as I heard the sadness and desperation in her voice, I tried to back away from admitting anything. I was too weak, too unsure of myself, too frightened of her, too frightened of what I might find if I opened my eyes and looked at life. She began yelling. Telling me what a bastard I was. Telling me how she didn't know me anymore. Asking me how I could live with myself. Telling me it was over. Telling me how she knew I was lying. Telling me to go to hell.

"I knew you were masturbating—that's why you were never interested in sex!" she screamed. I felt my spirit shriveling up inside of me. Sara began crying like a hurt child, a kind of bitter weeping that I had never heard before. She curled up into a ball, weeping and moaning as if this deep wound within her had been opened and could never be sewn together again.

I was sitting on the floor just ten feet away from her, stunned. I ran my hands through my hair, wanting to cry. But nothing came. I felt like I might throw up. I must have listened to her cry for thirty minutes, and as I did, I kept saying, "Sara, I'm so sorry. I love you. Let's talk about this." It became almost a mantra as I repeated it again and again: "I'm so sorry ... I love you ... I'm so sorry ... I love you."

She kept crying on the floor. I had no idea what to do, but I felt as if I needed to comfort her, to try to understand what she was feeling. So I got up to touch her shoulder, and as I reached down, she screamed at me.

"Get away from me! I don't even know you anymore!"

Sara left that night, and in some ways, she never came back. She didn't know where she was going, but she couldn't stay.

She couldn't stand to be near me. She grabbed a duffel bag and began throwing clothes into it. In less than five minutes, she was gone. I stood at the window and watched her red car drive into the night; I watched until her taillights disappeared.

The evening began in such an ordinary way and ended in misery and terror. That night something inside Sara broke. It was something intangible, yet something so significant that Sara would never be the same again. What broke was her trust in me, but perhaps it was much more than that; perhaps it was her trust in providence, her trust in God, her trust in what was good and pure and holy. Maybe what broke was something already broken—a wound reopened, a wound she had never mentioned because she was too ashamed, too hurt, or simply unaware of it.

After her car was out of sight, I stood at the window, not knowing what to do with myself. I couldn't call my parents; I couldn't call my friends—I wouldn't have known what to say or how to admit that I was less than what they thought I was. So I finally took a shower and went to bed. I cried that night as I slept in bed alone, but tears came only in short bursts. I was just as wounded as Sara, but I suspected her wound was a raw, bleeding cut that had been reopened, originally caused by God knows what. My wound was a slow internal bleeding.

I fell asleep with the phone next to me. I knew that Sara must have taken the two-and-a-half-hour trip to see her parents. She was alone, driving in the dark in the middle of the night. I worried about her, but more than that, I worried about what the future held. She had never left before. What would happen? What would she tell her parents? How would I ever make it through this?

Hours later, my eyes opened as the phone rang. It was Sara, crying and angry. "What are you doing?" she asked sharply as I picked up the phone.

"I was just sleeping, hoping you would call," I said, extending my neck, squinting at the alarm clock. It was three in the morning.

"I don't know how you can sleep knowing what you've done to me," she said through her tears. She was sobbing.

After more yelling and crying, the conversation ended. I stared up at the ceiling for a while before closing my eyes. I prayed a small prayer. "God, help. Help." I lay there hoping to sink into a deep sleep, a sleep from which I might never wake.

Above my head hung a plaque that in elegant script proclaimed, "I have found the one whom my soul loves." It was a framed copy of our wedding invitation.

Dead Man Walking

The next day was Sunday. As I lay in bed—eyes open, staring at the same white ceiling—I realized that my entire body ached. I felt as if I had just played a game of tackle football and was on the losing end of a lopsided contest. I didn't want to move; I didn't want to breathe; and most of all, I didn't want to face the fact that my marriage had just suffered a blow from which it might never recover.

I weighed my options. I could stay in bed, but I doubted I would fall back asleep. I could call a friend and recount what had happened, but that would mean admitting defeat, admitting that I was less than perfect.

The only thing that made sense was to go to church. I didn't want to go, but part of me clung to hope, thinking maybe someone at church could help. I also knew that I needed to pray, and church seemed like the best place to do that. Of course, I could've prayed in my apartment, but my apartment felt cursed. It felt like a place of anti-prayer—a place where prayers went to die, a place where prayers bounced off ceilings and back onto the ground. I wanted to be somewhere holy, yet even church didn't feel holy. The megachurch I attended felt more like a convention center filled with shiny, happy people than a holy cathedral where sinful, repentant people went to meet with God. But I wasn't about to begin looking for a new church to attend that morning.

As I got into my car, I felt hung-over. My hands were shaking as I gripped the steering wheel. While driving, I realized this would be the first time I had ever gone to church without Sara since we were married. It also became clear to me that we had been going there for more than a year and didn't know anyone in the congregation, let alone any of the pastors. I wanted so badly to talk to a pastor—someone in authority who would tell me that everything would be okay, that I was a good person, that Sara was crazy, that they would get her help.

As I neared the church, I turned on the radio and found a Christian radio station. I needed something hopeful, some-thing to hold onto—I needed a word from God. Shortly after I turned it on, I heard these lyrics: "Never underestimate my Jesus ... when the world around you crumbles, he will be strong ..." I felt tears rolling down my cheeks. "No, Jesus, I won't underes-timate You," I prayed. "I am weak, but You are strong. Please be strong. Please. My world has crumbled."

I have no idea what the sermon was about that day. I sat in the balcony, just another face in the crowd, blankly staring at the pastor. I could hardly sing any of the hymns.

I waited around after the service, hoping to talk to one of the pastors. I spotted a pastor, but someone was talking to him. I waited. And then someone else grabbed his attention and began talking to him. After about ten minutes, I finally left. I walked back to my car with no one to put their arm around me, no one to talk to. As I made my way through the enormous parking lot, thousands of well-dressed churchgoers spilled out of the megachurch, climbing into their SUVs and minivans, completely unaware of me.

It struck me how selfish we are, how alone we can feel even when we're in the midst of thousands. I felt completely hopeless, yet I kept thinking, "Never underestimate my Jesus."

Dad, Can You Help?

"Dad, do you have a second?" I asked.

"Sure, son, what's up?" my dad said from the other end of the phone.

I had just returned from church, and I needed help. Faced with my first full day without Sara, I needed someone to connect with on a deep level; I needed someone to share my pain. I couldn't bury it for much longer.

"Sara left last night. She was upset, and she just left. I'm really scared."

He asked if I wanted him to drive up and see me, and I said

yes. Two hours later, my dad was sitting with me in my apartment. There was a baseball game on television. We watched it and talked about our favorite team for a while. My dad and I had always connected with sports, which is one reason I still love sports today. Sports meant time with dad. Sports meant talking with dad. Sports meant trips to the old Tiger Stadium in Detroit: left-field upper-deck box seats, a clear midsummer evening, my dad pointing out the art of the double steal and the hit-and-run and the sacrifice bunt. I remember clear fall evenings in the driveway, playing basketball with my dad, my dad shooting left-handed jump shots that were sometimes swatted away by the branches from an evergreen tree that overwhelmed our backboard. I remember watching Michael Jordan and the Bulls face Isaiah Thomas and the Pistons at a playoff game in Detroit, my dad and I yelling and booing and cheering with twenty thousand other fanatics.

But talking about something like this—about Sara leaving and why she left—was foreign territory for us, so naturally we started with sports. But as the minutes passed, I felt a growing urgency to tell him what happened, especially because Sara could return at any minute. I expected her to return later that evening, but I really had no idea. As I told my dad what happened, he nodded and listened without question or comment.

When I was done with my story, he asked for a Bible. He turned to a well-known passage about love. "Love is patient. Love is kind. Love keeps no record of wrongs." He started talking about grace, about forgiveness, about how marriage has its ups and downs. I was almost frustrated by how calm he seemed.

He then asked if I had eaten lunch. I hadn't. So he took me to a nearby restaurant, and even though I wasn't hungry, I ordered a sandwich, and so did he. And as we ate, we talked about sports.

A Terrible Dream?

Sara didn't look at me when she returned late Sunday evening but headed straight for our room and locked the door behind her. After a few minutes, I walked over to the door and tried to talk to her—tried to ask her if there was anything I could do or if there was anything we needed to talk about. She said nothing. I stood there for a moment, my head leaning against the door, listening. It sounded like she was putting her clothes away, but it was hard to tell.

I slept on the couch that night and for the next few nights after that. I tried to work on freelance writing assignments during the day, but I was expending so much emotional energy worrying about Sara, worrying about my marriage, worrying about what was going to happen that I could hardly focus on anything other than her.

The days following Sara's return were so muddied, so sad, so strange that now they resemble a terrible dream—the kind where you forget the details immediately after waking up. All you remember is that someone died and it was your fault. As I slept on the couch, I remember how every noise coming from our bedroom made me jumpy. I remember feeling that at any moment Sara might come storming out with more accusations.

I remember how it felt to have Sara refuse to talk to me for days on end. Every evening when Sara returned home, the silence constantly punished me, bullied me, slowly stripping me of whatever it was that made me human. I felt as if I didn't exist—at least not in her eyes. The silence was a dripping faucet, slowly eating away at my soul, wearing away the edges, love turning to rust, as Bono sings in "Where the Streets Have No Name."

One day after Sara had left for work, I took a shower and got dressed, preparing myself for a day of writing. As I walked into the dining room to grab a folder, I found Sara standing in the corner, back pressed against the wall, glaring at me. I was taken by complete surprise and yelled, "What are you doing!?"

I don't remember what she said. She might have said nothing at all. But Sara had made her point: She was watching me. I had better be careful. She was not going to be taken advantage of. Things were different now. There was hell to pay.

Get Out

One night, Sara started talking to me again. But she just wanted to talk about "my problem." The questions and accusations were all over the map. Some of them made me angry, but I remained calm and just let her vent. She sat on the bed while I stood in the doorway. For the most part, Sara was calm as she questioned me, though there was a fire just beneath the surface that seemed capable of consuming her at any moment.

It was clear from her interrogation that she thought I was a pervert. She asked how often I masturbated, where I masturbated, who I thought about. While I thought she was crazy, she had reason to be suspicious of me: I had lied to her in the past about many issues, including this one. She had accused me in the past of struggling with masturbation, and I always denied it, once to the point of "swearing to God" that it wasn't something I did.

Sara had also just found out about something that I had never told her. Her brother, who attended college with us, had recently told Sara that he had heard that while we were dating, I had cheated on her at a party—the one my theater honorary held the night I was inducted. Sara was horrified when I confirmed that yes, I had been drinking, and yes, I had kissed other girls at the party.

Sara started asking me about the women I had kissed, then about other women we went to college with and whether I found them attractive. Her mind was running a million miles an hour, paging through lists of questions, sorting through lists of things I had done or could have done or might have thought about doing.

"I know you must've found Kara attractive," she said. "You would—she's your type, isn't she? You like the nasty ones ... I should divorce you ... I'm going to do what you did to me. We'll see how you like it."

I once heard that "hurt people hurt people," and I believe that is true. Sara was not a horrible person. She had never been vindictive when we were dating. But she was so hurt, so wounded, that these accusations and threats came spilling out of her almost uncontrollably, as if there was a hole in her heart and she could no longer hold back what was inside.

In fact, Sara could no longer disguise the fact that she not only resented me, but that she couldn't live with me anymore. She saw what I had done as not just a series of indiscretions but as grounds for divorce. She quoted the Sermon on the Mount, where Jesus says that if any man lusts after a woman, he has committed adultery in his heart. She took this statement literally and felt justified in pursuing divorce if it should come to that. But in the meantime, she just wanted me out.

One day, she came home from work midmorning, threw a bag at my feet, and told me to leave.

"Are you serious?" I asked.

"Get out. Now," she said, her jaw tightening. I could tell that I was in no position to reason with her, so I threw as many pieces of clothing as I could in my bag and walked out the door. As the door closed, I heard Sara locking it behind me.

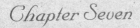

Chapter Seven

Losing Myself

You wanted to get somewhere so badly
You had to lose yourself along the way
You changed your name
Well that's okay, it's necessary
And what you leave behind
You don't miss anyway

—"Gone," U2

It was a beautiful spring day as I accelerated onto the highway. The sun was out, and temperatures were warmer than they had been in months. But despite the fact that the world was reborn—trees coming to life again, grass becoming greener—I hardly noticed. I was on the verge of a nervous breakdown.

My wife had just told me to get out of the apartment, and her

tone indicated that I might never be invited back. I had nowhere to go, no way to make sense of what was happening to
me, no way to patch things up with Sara. So I did the only thing
I could think of: I drove to my parents' house, an hour and a half
away. My mind was on autopilot. I was confused and scared.

While my mind was disengaged, my stomach was not. After
forty minutes on the highway, I pulled off and found a Taco
Bell. I also bought a *USA Today*, combing through the sports
section as I ate. It was strange that I was acting so calmly. I was
exhibiting the same sort of behavior that terminally ill patients
are sometimes known for—the sort of peace that marks those
who have come to accept that their best days are behind them
and, as a result, begin treasuring the smallest things in life.

Lunch was also a diversion. Diversions have always been my
specialty. In junior high, I kept thoughts of science tests at bay
by listening to baseball games on my clock radio as I drifted to
sleep. But test day always came, and the results were never pretty.

As I left the fast-food restaurant, "test day" had arrived, and it
appeared that I would once again fail. I have no memory of the
next hour, but I managed to find my way to my parents' driveway, and when I did, I sat there for what seemed like hours. I
didn't want to get out of the car; I didn't want to live. I kept
thinking about how my wife and I had pulled into that driveway dozens of times together, my right hand on her leg, my left
hand grasping the steering wheel. I now wondered if we would
ever again pull into that driveway together.

Defeated, I opened the car door and languidly walked into the
house. I took my bag to the guest room, throwing it on the
lower bunk. Sitting on the edge of the bed with my chin in my

hands, I noticed how the afternoon sun spilled near my feet. Everything was still.

I don't remember standing up, but I did because I eventually found my mom. I told her what had happened. It was one of the most humiliating experiences of my life: Detailing my struggles with lust, telling her that I had kissed other girls in college while dating Sara, telling her that I was kicked out and had nowhere to go, telling her that I didn't know if I was going to make it through this.

"Honey, a lot of people have struggled with these things—it's not that uncommon," my mom assured me. It was the same sort of assurance she gave me as a thirteen-year-old, when as an insecure adolescent, I told her through tears that I wasn't good at anything. She told me that I was. And here she was again, trying to assure me that I was okay. But I didn't feel like I was.

As my new life away from Sara began to take shape, my parents showered me with grace. They tried to be positive. They bought my favorite foods, made my favorite meals, tried to talk to me about how I was feeling and what I might do. They left books at my bedside on how to cope with separation and divorce. But despite their best efforts, nothing worked. None of these books spoke to me. Each book offered advice that didn't match reality as I knew it. My reality was stranger than fiction.

My reality consisted of the following: Not telling my parents too much about my relationship with Sara, not criticizing Sara in any way, not having lustful thoughts (or at least trying not to), not watching television alone, not going to the beach (or anywhere there might be attractive women), not contacting certain friends, and not forgetting to tell Sara every single one of my thoughts and actions.

I could feel Sara's nails digging into my neck. Her propensity to control me took on mythical proportions. I felt trapped in my own body, and I was constantly on guard—not only afraid that others might lead me astray, but afraid that I might lead myself astray. I policed myself as if my relationship with Sara hinged on my every thought and action. If my parents started to say anything critical of Sara, I would cringe and interrupt them. "Dad, you don't understand," I would protest. "It's not her fault. It's my fault—I'm the problem."

After a few weeks, Sara and I began talking again. I dreaded our conversations because she wanted to know everything that my parents said or tried to say. I would have to tell her all of the thoughts that I had, or might have had. If I didn't, she would threaten divorce. I began to feel that the weight of our relationship rested solely on my shoulders, and the burden became almost too heavy to carry.

My behavior became obsessive and unhealthy. I was desperate to impress Sara—desperate to prove my worth and win her back. The first thing I began doing was trying to avoid having any sort of sexual feeling. If I glanced up at the television and saw a woman in a bikini, I put myself through a rigorous self-examination: Did I enjoy that? Did I have a lustful thought? How long did I look at the woman? Was it too long? Did I look away as quickly as I could have? How would I explain this to Sara? And explain I would. I made a pact to literally tell Sara everything—from seeing a beautiful woman to having a thought about sex.

I knew that I couldn't live up to the impossible standard that Sara had set for me. I began reading every Christian book I could get my hands on. I would sit for hours on my parents' porch, reading my Bible or a book that outlined how to be a godly man. Sometimes I would take notes or write out resolutions or pray that I would stop being such a screwup. I would pray that Sara could somehow forgive me, that she could love someone as unlovable as me.

While I found myself growing spiritually—prayer became an essential part of my day—in some ways I was regressing spiritually. I began drifting into the seductive world of fundamentalism, locking myself away from the outside world, from the evil that seemingly lurked around every corner. I began focusing on what not to do, what not to touch, where not to go, what not to think about. I found myself placing the god of Sara alongside the God of Israel.

While I experienced genuine remorse, Sara was often my only motivation for change. And as saving my marriage became my goal, God became more of a genie in a bottle than anything else. I began fasting regularly, drinking only Gatorade, praying face-down on my knees.

I thought that if I committed myself to God completely, my marriage would be saved. What I didn't realize was that, in the process of "committing myself to God," I was losing any sense of the person that God created. My personality became somber, serious, wooden. The joy that I once had turned into a puritanical scowl—the byproduct of a deep depression I had fallen into. For someone who had become so religious, I lacked the "joy of the Lord."

On some level, it was to be expected that I would go through a period of mourning. Didn't King David do that very thing? Psalm 51 records David writing, "Have mercy on me, O God

... let me hear joy and gladness; let the bones you have crushed rejoice." David was trying to recover the joy he had lost after he committed adultery and murder. There was reason to be sad.

The joy of the Lord wasn't evident in those late days of May, sleeping in the bottom bunk of my parents' guest room. I would wake up and glance at the clock. If it was 10:30 a.m., I would roll over and fall back asleep. Ten- to twelve-hour nights of sleep became increasingly common. As a freelance writer, I worked when I felt like it, and throughout the end of May and on into June, I usually didn't feel like it. Work became secondary to simply getting through each day.

I remember sitting on the couch one Friday night. I had been emailing Sara, but things weren't going well. Most of her responses were a combination of anger and incredible sadness. She would talk about how I betrayed her in college, how I was a pervert. She would ask how I could live with myself.

I would read her emails and fire off quick, desperate replies filled with promises and oaths and Bible verses and any conceivable tactics I could think of to keep her from filing for divorce. "You don't understand—I really love you, Sara. You're all I think about, and I am doing so much better. I really have changed, even in this short period of time. I know it's hard to believe, but it's true. Our marriage and my relationship with God are the only things that matter. Please, let's work this out. Things will be so much better now. I love you so much ..."

Sara's replies were usually devastating critiques of what I had written. She would point out all of my past inconsistencies, all of the reasons why she doubted that I had changed. She would make tough accusations about how she knew I was keeping something from her.

That night as I sat on the couch with my brother's laptop, my parents sat nearby, watching television. My mom asked if there was anything that she could do, and I assured her there was nothing. My depression had lingered for weeks, and my mom could hardly stand it any longer. She began to cry. I didn't know whether to cry with her or lash out in anger.

"I don't know what to do," she said. "I don't know how to help you. I just don't want to see you so sad anymore. You've been through so much. You've been sad for so long."

I gave her a hug and told her that it was okay, that things would work out. But deep down, I didn't think that they would.

As I went to bed that night, I remembered my favorite Shakespearean sonnet—the one I had shared with Sara in a letter years ago.

> Weary with toil, I haste me to my bed,
> The dear repose for limbs with travel tired;
> But then begins a journey in my head
> To work my mind, when body's work's expired;
> For then my thoughts, from far where I abide,
> Intend a zealous pilgrimage to thee,
> And keep my drooping eyelids open wide,
> Looking on darkness which the blind do see:
> Save that my soul's imaginary sight
> Presents thy shadow to my sightless view,
> Which, like a jewel hung in ghastly night,
> Makes black night beauteous and her old face new.
> Lo, thus, by day my limbs, by night my mind
> For thee, and for myself, no quiet find.[1]

I Can't Hear You

Sara and I began having more and more phone contact, and eventually we began going to counseling together again. It was the same counselor we had gone to six months before with our in-law problems. The last time we saw him was only days after that night in the bookstore café when Sara left.

I don't remember driving the hour and a half from my parents' house; I don't remember what I felt when I saw Sara. But I do remember bits and pieces of our meeting with the counselor. I described how I had been living with my parents for the past month but wanted to reunite with Sara. Sara described with no small degree of horror how I had lied and convinced her that I was something much different than what I really was. She said that I couldn't be trusted, that I had an uncontrollable problem with masturbation and lust.

The counselor stoically evaluated the situation and began asking probing questions, occasionally scribbling notes on a legal pad. I remember him telling a story of someone who drove around looking at other women during his lunch break. He would lust and stare and touch himself. He eventually got caught exposing himself to one of these women. I'm not sure if the counselor told this story to put my problem in perspective for my wife—"look, he's not as bad as that"—or if he told it to frighten her—"look, he needs more counseling or this is what could happen to him."

Sara seemed to go for the latter—she embraced the idea that I was in need of serious help. In fact, she seemed frightened of me. She pointed to other men that she looked up to, including her dad and brothers, as if to say, "These are men of integrity. These are men who would never do what you did." I insisted that they too had likely struggled with lust, but she would have none of it. She was convinced that I was abnormal, perverted, and unlikely to be rehabilitated.

Our counseling sessions were weekly, but very little counseling was done there. Mostly, the counselor would listen as my wife wrestled with the rage that she felt toward me. I would make the three-hour-roundtrip drive to hear my wife say frightening things like "I'm not sure if I can go on like this," "I'm not sure I want to be married to someone like him," "I wish I never would've married him."

During one of our sessions, at the prompting of my wife, the counselor asked me to fill out a form that would diagnose the extent of my problems with lust. Weeks later, the counselor told us that I was not a sexual addict as my wife had suspected, but that perhaps I had some of the same addictive tendencies.

My wife and I disagreed many times about what the counselor said on that day, but that is how I very clearly remember it. Sara continued to insist that I had a sexual addiction, and I would furrow my brow and roll my eyes every time she said it.

One of the last times we saw the counselor was when—after detailing my struggles over the course of several appointments—he asked if there was anything else I wanted to tell Sara. He insisted that if there was anything else that I needed to tell her, it had better be done by our next meeting.

That week was one of the longest of my life. I prayed and prayed. I called my best friend, asking for advice. My closet had two other skeletons of which my wife knew nothing about. There was that time in Cancun on a hormone-propelled floating nightclub that I kissed a girl after knowing her for about twenty minutes. The alcohol helped me justify cheating on Sara. And there was one other time after a booze-filled college party—also while dating Sara—that I allowed a girl to get closer, much closer, than I should have. I thought these two incidents might be the death of our marriage, and I wondered if it would be better to tell Sara at all, judging by her reaction to the things I had already told her.

Of course, I had excuses. Both times I had been drinking. And both events happened long before we were engaged and long before I started following Jesus. But those were just excuses, and I knew they would hold little weight with my wife, who knew much more about truth-telling than grace-giving.

After much thought and prayer, I decided to tell Sara everything. Of course, I didn't go into detail, and I left enough out so it sounded better than it probably was.

As I recounted the stories in the counselor's office, Sara reacted stoically. Her face was pale. She nodded, her eyes locked on mine. Her eyes seemed determined, as a teacher is determined to not allow a disruptive student to frustrate her anymore.

At the end of the session, Sara said that she didn't think she needed to attend counseling anymore. She said that I was the one in need of counseling. I didn't disagree with her—I was in no position to.

It's My Fault

I continued to make the three-hour-roundtrip drive each week, but it always saddened me that Sara was not there. It was difficult to climb the staircase to the counselor's office—each step sorrowful, each step a reminder that I was alone.

I usually arrived ten minutes early. Sweating nervously, I'd head for the bathroom before entering the counselor's suite. Sometimes I would stand at the sink and splash cold water on my face, drying it with a paper towel as I stared in the mirror. I wasn't always sure who was looking back at me. Taking a deep breath, I'd gather my courage and head into the counselor's office. And yes, it took courage. Sitting with a man who I hardly knew, pouring out my deepest secrets, handing him my shame—it was never something that came easily.

Thankfully, someone made it easier, at least in some small, almost imperceptible way. The receptionist had kind eyes and a sympathetic soul. She always greeted me by name—"Hi, Cameron, good to see you today"—as I signed in at the front desk. Months later, she told me that she was praying for me before I went in for a particularly important day of counseling. As playwright Tennessee Williams once wrote, "I have always relied on the kindness of strangers." This woman was one of them.

Whenever I took a seat in the waiting room, I tried to avoid glancing at the magazines that were tossed on end tables and chairs. As someone who has always loved news—and loved to read—this was like asking Mr. Universe not to touch the exercise equipment in the weight room. Glancing at a magazine could kill my marriage—my wife had told me so—and I was determined not to be destroyed by something so simple and innocuous. Sometimes I would bring a book with me; other times I would simply look at the floor or up at the ceiling while I waited. I never questioned this because I was so plagued by guilt. I was convinced that I had to be punished—perhaps for the rest of my life. If this was my punishment, I would accept it.

Once in the counselor's office, I was still ill at ease. Holding a

Styrofoam cup filled with bad coffee, I often hoped that our small talk would last the entire hour, yet I also hoped that I might somehow leave feeling encouraged, renewed, and enlightened.

The counselor was a kind man, but I imagine that even the kindest, most sympathetic people have their limits. I sometimes wondered how much complaining he had to endure each day. And I often wondered if my sessions sounded like complaining to him as I sat on his dark leather couch.

I didn't complain as much as I pleaded for him to understand where I was coming from, to acknowledge my pain, to acknowledge that I wasn't as bad as my wife said I was. But the counselor preferred to focus on what I was "learning."

I was supposed to be learning from my mistakes, but I didn't particularly care about anything other than getting my wife back. Nevertheless, the counselor forced me to evaluate my entire life, especially why I shied away from intimacy with my wife and why I resorted to unhealthy behaviors to try to meet some sort of deep aching in my soul. I had assignments: books to read, questions to ponder, lists to make.

I suppose that I learned some things about myself, but I didn't learn how to escape the shame that lingered, which was becoming increasingly unhealthy. Shame seemed to envelop every part of my being. I had trouble defining what was real and what wasn't, and the counselor never seemed to help.

I wanted him to answer simple questions: Am I crazy or is my wife crazy? Is my wife responding strangely to this situation? Is there something seriously wrong with me? Why can't I seem to do anything right? How can I please my wife when I'm already doing everything possible to make things better?

The counselor didn't like to answer questions such as these; he preferred to ask them. I wanted answers, but everywhere I looked I found only more questions.

The Answers

We finally found someone who had answers. He was a counselor recommended to us by a friend, and his instruction manual was the Bible. He spoke with a bit of a Southern accent, and we first met him in a small office around the corner from a sign that read "Jesus Saves." This counselor was the pastor of a small nondenominational church, and as part of his ministry, he spent time counseling married couples.

The first time Sara and I met him was on a ninety-degree day in July. I was hopeful and very nervous, so I gave myself plenty of time to get there. I left my parents' house at 2:30 p.m. for the 5:00 p.m. appointment. But I didn't anticipate running into traffic or construction, and as it turned out, that was a big mistake.

A section of the highway that I routinely took was down to one lane. Yellow construction equipment and orange cones littered the landscape. Standstill traffic magnified the potholes and glaring sunlight, jackhammers and barrels, honking horns and people kissing in the car in front of me.

I turned up the radio—someone on a news program was yelling about the hot political issues of the day. Sweat dripped down my face as traffic stood still and tires melted into the pavement. Minutes became a half-hour, and a half-hour an hour.

By the time I made my way through the construction war zone, I realized that I would be lucky to make the appointment at all. Fortunately, I had my parents' cell phone, so I began calling the counseling center furiously. But the center had no secretarial help, so my calls were cycled into an automated system. I spoke several times into what seemed like a voicemail abyss, doubtful if anyone was getting my messages.

Finally, I called again. Twenty minutes too late, the counselor answered the phone. "Yes, get here as soon as you can. Yes, she's here. Yes, okay. See you soon."

As I hung up the phone, I began to cry. A day earlier I had told Sara that I would be on time. The fact that I was now late was just one more nail in my coffin, one more example that I didn't care, one more indication that I wasn't willing to put the effort into making our marriage work.

I pulled into the counseling center and ran toward the front door. I was forty-five minutes late. Out of breath, I grabbed a seat and explained once again the terrible construction and traffic.

The counselor, Mike, had gray hair and a mustache and was wearing a checkered, short-sleeved shirt. He handed me a Bible and told me to open to some passage. Sara already had her Bible open.

He briefly took us through a passage about marriage that seemed completely irrelevant—about how God created Adam and Eve, how Eve was created from Adam's rib because God said that it was not good for man to be alone.

At some point, he also asked Sara to recap why we were there, and then he wanted me to offer my explanation. It was obvious that he and Sara had covered this topic thoroughly before I arrived, so there wasn't much for me to add.

He then explained that the counseling center did not charge but asked for donations. After going through a pamphlet that explained the center's donation policy, we scheduled our next appointment with him.

Standing in the parking lot, I watched Sara walk toward her car—our car—without saying anything. I moved closer and apologized for being late. I told her about the traffic, and as I did, I started to cry. I told her that I missed her so much, that I was so tired of doing this.

Sara's glare bore a hole through my head. Her jaw was set, her shoulders tense. I wanted to follow her home—back to our apartment, back to where my things were, back to the place I was supposed to be—but that wouldn't happen. Sara was too angry.

A Patchwork Quilt

It's difficult to remember anything from the three months that I lived with my parents. Some scenes are too painful to remember; others have simply been forgotten.

My memories of Sara are like a patchwork quilt—different scenes, different times all bound together by threads of sadness. I am at a loss to recall where the different pieces came from—how I found them, how they fit together, or why some scenes are a part of my quilt and others are not.

For our wedding, a friend gave us a beautiful handmade quilt of blue pieces of fabric. The back of the quilt read, "Love covers over a multitude of sins ..."

Today, the quilt is stuffed in a closet. It is too beautiful to throw away and too painful to keep. How can a quilt intended for something so good now represent something so painful? The verse on the back is a study in irony. Love didn't cover over a multitude of sins. There wasn't enough love, or the right kind of love, or maybe any love.

When I look at the quilt, I don't think of the beauty of marriage or the beauty of love. I think of hate. I think of betrayal. I think of emptiness. Sadly, our marriage wasn't bound by all of the beautiful things the quilt portrayed. Instead, it was bound only by selfishness—mine and Sara's.

And because of that, the quilt will never be displayed at fiftieth wedding anniversary parties or handed down to grandchildren. The quilt will never symbolize bonds of matrimony, but strange memories of a destroyed love affair—a marriage remembered only in the deep recesses of broken hearts, or in the backs of closets or attics where unwanted things are stored.

Chapter Eight

Alone in
the World

Don't move, don't talk out-a time
Don't think, don't worry
Everything's just fine, just fine
Don't grab, don't clutch
Don't hope for too much ...
I feel numb

—"Numb," U2

It was a Saturday morning in a crowded restaurant—clinking silverware, laughter at the next table, and midmorning sun streaming through the windows. Across from me sat Jeff, whom I had met only minutes earlier. I had driven an hour and a half to ask Jeff whether I could live in his house for a few weeks or maybe even a few months.

Sara had given me Jeff's phone number. He was a friend of one of Sara's coworkers. Jeff was tall, in his early thirties, and a youth pastor at a local church. Being single and a follower of Jesus, Jeff routinely let people stay in the guest room of his house for weeks or months at a time. Jeff loved helping hurting people— people just like me. And it showed in how he lived his life.

Sara and our marriage counselor had encouraged me to move out of my parents' house, and I reluctantly agreed. I was reluctant because I had nowhere else to go. I knew virtually no one. But there I was, an hour and a half away from my parents' house, talking to a stranger, preparing to move closer to Sara despite the fact that I had no guarantee that she would ever take me back. I knew it was the right thing to do, yet I dreaded being completely alone with no support system.

"So tell me about your situation," Jeff said after our food arrived. My eggs turned cold as I launched into the story. I rehashed the painful events that led me to where I was now: alone, scared, and sitting in a restaurant looking for a place to live. Jeff nodded reassuringly, calmly eating his breakfast as I spoke.

After I had finished my story, Jeff looked up from his food and started talking.

"A lot of guys have struggled with the things you're describing ... I mean, I was worried that you had had an affair or something," Jeff said. Reading between the lines, I felt as if Jeff was saying, "You should be able to work this out with Sara ... this isn't the end of the world." We talked further, and our breakfast meeting ended with Jeff telling me that he would think about everything and give me a call next week.

That next week, Jeff called and told me that I was welcome to stay at his house. I thanked him and said that I would plan on moving later that week, after my midweek counseling appointment with Sara.

One Month of Silence

"Have you come to any decisions yet, Sara?" the counselor asked from his leather chair. "Is this marriage going to work?"

I could feel my heart thumping. I was terrified of what Sara would say. I imagined it would be something along the lines of "No, it's not going to work. I'm done." As Sara pondered the question, my mind ran wild. For a few moments, there was only silence. And then finally: "I need a month with no contact," she said.

"Okay, well if that's what you feel like you need, let's meet again in a month. But I want you to make a decision by next month about whether or not you're going to continue in this relationship," the counselor said.

Sara nodded.

Sara and I had recently taken another step backward in our relationship, which is why she needed a month away from me. One week earlier, I had lied to Sara. The situation seemed innocent enough. My friend Kevin learned that I was separated from Sara. After I shared my story with him on the phone, he offered to take a week's vacation and spend some time with me—praying, talking, doing whatever I needed. I enthusiastically agreed to the idea. I was anxious for someone to listen, pray, help—until I told Sara.

"I don't think it's a good idea at all," Sara said. "You have to make your own decisions, but I don't think it's a good idea."

Looking back on it, I don't even remember why Sara didn't want him to come—she just didn't. The next day, just before Kevin was prepared to drive several hundred miles to see me—his bags were already packed—I called him. It was early in the morning.

"Hello."

"Hey, Kevin. It's Cameron. Sorry to call so early … it's just that … well, I just talked to Sara last night, and she really doesn't think that it's a good idea for you to come. I'm sorry … I just can't have you come. I don't want to upset her. I can't afford to upset her—the stakes are too high. I can't get into it … I just really can't talk to you about it."

Later that day, Sara called to see how I had handled the situation. "So, did you talk to Kevin?" she asked.

"Yeah, I did. I told him not to come."

"Well, what did you say?" Sara wondered.

"I just said that it wasn't a good time for him to come."

"You didn't say anything about me? You didn't say that I was the one who didn't want him to come?" she asked.

"No. No. I didn't say anything about you."

"You're lying. I can tell. You're lying to me right now. Unbelievable, but you are—you're lying."

There was no way to work myself out of this one. Once Sara had something in her mind, there was no convincing her otherwise—especially not now, now that she had been lied to and fooled and robbed of so many things that neither of us fully understood.

"Yes. You're right. I'm sorry, Sara ... I shouldn't have just said that. I lied. I told Kevin that you didn't want him to come ... that was so stupid. I'm so sorry, Sara ... I don't know what I was thinking ..."

"I told you, Cameron, that if you ever lied to me again, ever, we were done. Was there anything confusing about that?"

"Sara, I know ... please, let's talk about this ... I'm so sorry ... I wasn't thinking, and then you just asked me about it, and I totally freaked out because all of a sudden I could tell you were going to be really upset with my answer."

"Cam, stop. I'm not having this conversation. I can't believe you. I really can't believe you. I just don't know if this is going to work. I'm going to go."

In the days that immediately followed, I began searching the Internet for mental clinics that I could check myself into. All of them were quite expensive, but I was seriously considering it. I didn't know what else to do with myself. I felt defective.

Fast-forward a week later to the counselor's office where Sara said that she wouldn't speak to me for a month. After the session, in the parking lot, I approached her and tried to talk.

"Sara, I just want you to know that I love you, and I'm not giving up on us," I said. "I'm moving into Jeff's house today ...

so I'll be there. I guess you know how to contact me if there's an emergency or something. I'm really going to miss you. I feel so upset right now ... I mean, I can understand how you need some time, but a month is a lot ..."

Sara stood at a distance—six feet away—and stared at me, virtually expressionless. She then switched the topic and began questioning me about how much freelance work I had been doing lately, how much money I was making. "You're hardly doing anything lately, you're making virtually no money! What are you doing? You better think about getting another job. I'm not going to be married to someone who isn't ..."

I tuned her out. I began to stare into space. I was looking directly at Sara, but I wasn't looking at her at all. I was looking through her. I saw her mouth moving, but there was no sound. There were only my thoughts; there was only pain. I didn't know how much more I could take. She was right—I hadn't been getting much work lately. Most days, it was just an accomplishment to get through the day. Work had definitely taken a back seat to life, and I hardly cared about anything other than saving my marriage.

As I climbed into my car, I was defeated in almost every way possible. It was a bad night to move into a stranger's house.

My So-Called Life

I found Jeff's house, which was located on the other end of town. It was a one-story starter home. There was a small lake across the street with a grassy picnic area that I instantly thought would make a great place to pray and reflect. I parked my car and walked up to the front door. Jeff showed me the guest room and helped me carry some of my things in from the car. I didn't have much—a couple bags of clothes, a Bible, several books, a sleeping bag, and a large desktop computer.

The guest room was simple, but it had everything that I needed. It had a desk where I could put my computer and a mattress where I could sleep. There was also a small fan since the house didn't have air conditioning.

After getting situated, I went to the grocery store. Jeff said that I could store all of my food in his kitchen and that I was welcome to use things like ketchup and mayonnaise so that I didn't have to buy my own. With Sara's complaints about money on my mind, I tried to restrict my spending. I tried to buy a week's worth of groceries for $30 or less, which I managed by purchasing some frozen meals that were on sale.

As I walked through the grocery store, my heart was heavy and sad. I felt as if I could start crying at any moment. I wondered how I was even functioning. I was flatlining emotionally. I was almost dead.

When I got back to the house, I was anxious to talk to Jeff, anxious to simply have someone around. But Jeff informed me that he was going on vacation for a few days and was leaving in an hour. So I had the house to myself.

A thunderstorm was roaring as I went to sleep that night. I prayed that God would help me to become something someday, help me to become someone who mattered, someone who wasn't so selfish, so stupid. I wanted to become someone who wasn't so much like ... me.

Time to Think

I can't even begin to describe the month of silence. It's almost too painful.

If I were to explain everything that I did and felt, it would probably be the most painful part of the book for me to write. This part of the story could be a book in and of itself, and a pretty sad and boring one at that.

This section will be short and fast, though the month of silence was anything but short and fast. Here are the highlights:

I doubled my freelance writing efforts in an attempt to impress Sara with the amount of money that I could make in a month. (I didn't make that much money.)

On several occasions I talked to my best friend's mom, who had been through a divorce. She was my lifeline in some ways.

I didn't call my parents because I knew that Sara would be upset if I did. Sara said that I shouldn't try to rely on other people to ease my pain. So I tried to deal with everything on my own, with the exception of talking to my friend's mom.

I spent hours by the lake reading my Bible and other Christian books and praying.

I spent Saturday evenings wandering around a local Christian bookstore, not daring to go into a secular bookstore for fear that Sara wouldn't approve.

I attended a two-day Christian men's convention by myself. I cried whenever any of the speakers talked about marriage.

I started attending the church where Jeff was a pastor. One evening I went to a prayer service where a man laid hands on me.

I went to a store and bought a small frame, in which I placed a marriage "covenant" that I had written to Sara. I was planning on handing her the covenant when I saw her again at our next counseling session.

The Moment of Decision

Fast-forward one month to the counselor's office. I was seated in a chair across the room from Sara. The counselor sat in his large leather chair, his legs crossed, pensively looking at us.

"Well, is there anything that either of you wants to say before we get started?" the counselor asked. Before Sara had a chance to say anything, I presented her with the framed marriage covenant that I had written. I also gave her a bouquet of flowers. Our counselor was more impressed with the gifts than Sara was, but she smiled and quietly thanked me.

Sara had made her decision. She would stay in the relationship, but she still needed a lot of time. She wanted to see how the time apart had affected me, and she was willing to give our relationship another shot to see if I had changed. I was relieved and incredibly thankful, but I still felt uneasy because Sara's tone was quite reserved. She kept using terms like "one more shot," which made me realize that any misstep on my part might lead to divorce papers.

I kept thinking that it would be a matter of weeks before Sara and I got back together, but I remained at Jeff's house for more than two months before Sara let me return to the apartment.

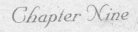

Chapter Nine

Look Straight Ahead

I'm a man, I'm not a child
A man who sees
The shadow behind your eyes

—"Kite," U2

In some ways our reunion was even more painful than our separation. Sara tried so hard to make things work, but my past mistakes continued to take their toll. In Sara's eyes, my credibility was as low as it could get. She always had high expectations, but in light of our problems her expectations felt overwhelming, especially after I moved back into our apartment.

A marriage counselor once told me he had a mental picture of me running around on a football field while Sara sat in the stands yelling: "Run left! Stop. Run right! Do some pushups!

Stop. Start running again!" And I would do as she commanded, certain that one day she would be pleased with my performance.

But that day never came.

In Sara's eyes, I could never do enough. Maybe it was because she was too hurt to let go of the past. Or maybe I was too naïve. I expected years of mistakes to be erased in a flash, but years of mistakes take years of healing. Unfortunately, healing never seemed to happen for Sara and me—all that seemed to happen was constant picking at a fresh scab.

I felt forever trapped in a moment from six months ago: Sara curled up on the floor crying like a wounded child, me placing my hand on her back, Sara yelling, "Don't touch me! I don't even know you anymore!" As I moved back into the apartment, it felt as if nothing had changed, as if we had never moved past that terrible night.

Be Quiet

Sara would often punish me with silence, which shouldn't have surprised me. Sara's mom used the same tactic to punish her husband. I remember Sara once telling me that her mom hadn't talked to her dad for an entire week after an argument.

As the months passed, Sara's resentment grew, and my attempts at conversation were increasingly met with silence. Sometimes the silence lasted for twenty minutes, other times an hour, and sometimes for an entire day or two. I think this actually made me try harder to please Sara, and in trying I almost lost myself.

Sometimes I would pray with Sara—not because I wanted to but because I couldn't think of anything else to do that would help our marriage. She would usually scoff at my attempts. Or she would say, "You can pray, but I'm not praying. I'm not saying anything." I would pray. And nothing would happen. Actually, things would usually get worse. Maybe that was the answer to my prayer, I don't know.

Sara said very little for two years, but in saying little she said so much. She said that she was hopeless. She said that she was angry. She said that there was a lot she couldn't leave behind.

The silence made me realize that the loneliest people in the world are not those who live alone; the loneliest people in the world are those who have a loved one who has stopped loving them back. I knew this was true, because I couldn't have been lonelier than I was when I was with Sara.

Sara had unplugged the television because she didn't trust me. Of course, removing the television made me feel even more isolated, it made me feel like even more of a pervert. My wife didn't even trust me in the house with a television. What had happened to me, to her, to us?

In order to silence the voices inside—the voices that screamed with rage—I retreated to the world of sports. I would listen to every baseball, football, and basketball game on the radio. It wasn't uncommon for me to spend most of a Saturday lying on the couch while staring at the white wall in front of me, listening to sports on the radio. Sometimes I would stay there for six or seven hours at a time. I could think of nothing better to do. I had very few friends in town, and my friends from college had quickly faded after Sara and I married.

As I lay on the couch, I occasionally wanted to do something.

Sometimes I would propose an outing to Sara—dinner, a visit to the museum, a drive to the lake. But doing anything together or going anywhere brought a tremendous amount of grief for her. Whenever we did go somewhere, Sara was likely to accuse me of something, or I was likely to notice something that Sara wouldn't want me to notice.

Driving home to see my parents was also out of the question. Sara would be upset or would grill me about what my parents had said about her while I was there. And my parents were bound to say something about Sara while I was there—they were too concerned not to say something. And if I didn't tell Sara what they said when I returned, I was automatically branded a liar. I would be in danger of losing Sara, who had threatened to leave if I ever lied to her again. So I never went.

Lying on the couch with my small clock radio and a book in my lap was the safest thing I could do. I sometimes wondered if it would always be like this, if I would live the rest of my life in fear and anxiety, waiting to be yelled at or avoided or ignored or left.

Feeling Like a Loser

I began to forget who I was aside from the person that Sara said I was. For the most part, I stopped laughing, stopped dreaming, stopped expecting anything to turn out well. I began to confuse love for Sara with self-loathing. Sometimes the only thing that seemed to appease Sara was when I would criticize myself, and I did that often. I avoided doing or saying anything that would upset Sara, even if it was something healthy, such as calling a friend. I accepted it as part of the punishment that someone as bad as I deserved.

What I didn't realize at the time—what Sara didn't realize—was that she was just as broken as I was. That didn't absolve me of my mistakes and their consequences, but it did mean that grace should've been more readily offered. But there was never enough grace.

As the months passed, Sara refused to even touch me. My hugs were often met with indifference or sometimes even revulsion. The girl who once hugged me so wholeheartedly was gone. But while the lack of physical contact hurt, the accusations hurt more. Because she had such little trust in me, Sara would constantly accuse me of anything and everything. Nothing I said was taken at face value.

This meant that I had to tell Sara every single thing I did during the day and recount any thought I had that she might deem inappropriate. This went on for months, and every day was exhausting—the pressure to remember, the pressure to tell, the pressure of forever think about not thinking.

I was constantly terrified that Sara would accuse me of not telling her everything about my day, which happened often. "You're not telling me everything. I can tell," Sara would say, staring me down coldly. Even worse, I was terrified that I would have some kind of lustful thought that I would have to recount once I returned from my new job at a newspaper. Sometimes, in recounting such a thought, I was brought to tears as Sara would stare blankly. She made me feel like a pervert, and I sometimes wondered if I struggled with lustful thoughts more than usual because my entire life revolved around not thinking them.

Life felt heavy. I always felt like damaged goods. I was constantly ashamed of myself, and especially ashamed around Sara. I think

Sara worried that if she didn't keep me in my place, I would hurt her again, and she couldn't stand the thought of that. So she never let me forget that I was bad, that I had hurt her, that I couldn't be trusted.

I will never forget walking through the grocery store with Sara, afraid to look up, afraid that she might accuse me of looking at other women.

"Sara, I'm staring at the ground, and it's pretty hard to walk around like this," I said once as I pushed the shopping cart.

"Why? You don't have to keep your head down, just keep your eyes on the floor," she said.

"I'm trying ... it's just difficult," I said.

"It shouldn't be that difficult," she said.

Just a few weeks earlier, Sara had accused me of glancing at a picture of a woman in a bikini. The picture was on the packaging for an inflatable raft.

"I saw you look at that picture," she said, her jaw tightening.

"Yes, I saw it—but I wasn't trying to look at it, Sara. Give me a break ... when I saw it, I looked away."

"I'm not buying that for a second. We already walked down this aisle once, and I know you saw it then. You should have known where it was and avoided it when you walked by again!"

"Sara, it wasn't a problem! I wasn't looking for it. This is so ridiculous. You can't trust me with anything. I don't know what to do."

I was exasperated. It had gotten to the point where I rarely struggled with the sorts of things I was being accused of, but Sara treated me as if I were a pornographer. I felt like I could hardly breathe around her.

Christmas Eve

Sara no longer wanted me around her family, and after our reunion I rarely saw them. I saw Sara's mom once in two years, and I never saw her father again.

During the holidays, Sara insisted that she go home alone, and she refused to see my family. I was so afraid of what Sara might think if I went home to see my parents for Christmas. On Christmas Eve, one day after Sara had left to see her family, I sat on the couch with the lights off. It was 9:00 p.m. and completely black outside. I sat there until 10:30, which is when I started to cry. I started to feel bad for myself, my situation, my marriage. But as quickly as I had started to cry, I stopped myself. I would not cry. I deserved this. This was my fault. Or so I thought.

I felt dead inside.

Finally, I packed a bag and drove to my parents' house. I hadn't had any contact with them for a week, and they had no idea that I was coming. My dad acted as if I was the prodigal son. "Kill the fatted calf," he said, laughing as I walked through the door. With my shoulders stooped, I forced a half-smile and tried to act happy. But happiness seemed a million miles off. Happiness seemed like something that I would never again feel.

"I'm Done"

I'll never forget the night Sara told me that she was done with marriage counseling forever. We had just returned from a meeting with the same counselor we had been seeing sporadically for almost a year. Thirty minutes earlier, Sara had walked out of the session when the counselor began asking questions about her unwillingness to ever see or talk to my mom again.

"I just won't put myself through that," Sara said.

"Do you ever think that you're reading into things? Do you ever wonder if you're misjudging her intentions?" the counselor asked, his head down, pen hovering over his legal pad.

"No. There's no way that I'm doing that. No way," Sara said firmly. She looked at me to back her up, but I said nothing.

"Sara, I'm not trying to upset you. I'm just asking the question," the counselor said, looking directly at Sara. "Isn't it possible that she's not as bad as you think she might be?" His voice was calm and gentle but firm. He had never asked Sara so many questions.

"Look. I'm not going to take this. This is ridiculous. I didn't come here for this," Sara said, her face turning pink. "I'm not going to sit here and listen to this; you don't even know the situation."

"I feel as if you're really upset right now, Sara," the counselor said calmly. "I can see that this is upsetting you. Why are you upset right now?"

"I'm done. I'm not doing this. I'm done," Sara said, fuming. She stood up and quickly walked out of the room. I sat there, shocked, looking at the counselor.

"Cam, I think you better go too," he said with a shrug of his shoulders.

I quickly walked out of the room and caught up with Sara, but she continued walking briskly down the stairs. "Sara, hold on; let's talk about this," I said.

"I'm done, Cam. I'm done."

"What do you mean you're done?" I asked, almost terrified that she would tell me she was filing for divorce.

"I'm done with counseling. It only makes things worse. And you—you—you are unbelievable," Sara said. "You totally know what your mom does, and you just sat there and said nothing. You didn't stick up for me at all. Unbelievable."

"Sara, I'm sorry, you're right, I should've stuck up for you ... I don't know what I was doing ... I'm sorry ... you're right," I said. "Please, Sara, let's talk. Please, don't run off so quickly." I wasn't even thinking about what I was saying; I just didn't want Sara to be upset. In fact, I was always terrified that Sara might get upset, and I spent so much time and energy trying not to irritate her.

Sara got in her car—we had driven separately—and sped off. I walked back up to the counselor's office and talked to him about what had happened.

"I don't know, Cam. I don't know what to say to you," he told me. "She's very angry. I don't quite understand it, but she's very angry."

As we spoke further about Sara, the counselor said something I'll never forget, something true, but at the time very hurtful: "You're just not a good match, Cam. The two of you are not a good match."

Going Home

One day, Sara got an email from her mom saying that something serious had happened. Sara needed to get home as soon as she could, the email said, so Sara left work early, talking to me in the apartment as she furiously threw clothes in a duffel bag.

"Did you call your mom?" I asked.

"Yes, but she wouldn't say what the problem was on the phone," she said. "It's really serious. She was crying."

I gave Sara a hug and told her to call me when she knew something.

That night, Sara called and told me that her parents were getting divorced. She was devastated. She looked at her parents' relationship as an example of a healthy marriage, and by most indications, it was. They had been married for twenty-five years.

After several days, Sara returned home and was even more reserved than usual. She didn't want to talk about what happened, but slowly the stories began to spill out. Maybe she told me because she had no one else to talk to. I was just glad that she was talking about anything. I tried to listen sympathetically and let Sara vent any frustrations or sadness that she was feeling, but Sara found me to be cold, detached, and unsympathetic. And maybe she was right. Maybe my response to the entire situation was mechanical. I was so wounded myself that it was difficult to feel anything for Sara.

I struggled to feel sympathy for Sara's parents, who had insisted not that long ago that she divorce me. Over time, Sara pulled back from any contact with me, saying that I couldn't be trusted, that I wasn't helping her deal with the situation, that I was only interested in myself.

"I would've hoped that you could see I'm going through the toughest time of my life! I would've hoped that you could be more sympathetic!" she said.

I felt terrible.

I told Sara that I loved her and wanted to help her. And I did still love Sara even if I wasn't in love with her.

As the oldest child and her mom's confidant, Sara was on the phone every day for hours at a time trying to make sense of the pain, hurt, and confusion, trying to be a rock for her mom, who was typically the steady one. I knew that Sara felt drained. She had recently confronted her dad, and through tears he talked to her.

Sara's dad was now out of the picture, but he was still living in the same house with her mom. No one in the family was communicating with him, other than for business purposes. Sara felt as if a piece of her had died. She had always loved and respected her father so much; she had always wanted to marry someone just like him. But as she learned more about her dad's past and the mistakes he had made, she felt like she *had* married him.

The things that her dad did began to color how Sara viewed me, and not just me, but men in general. She began making negative comments about men, and I could clearly see why she would feel that way. The two men she had trusted the most, the two men who she thought would never hurt her had both hurt her beyond anything she had ever experienced before.

I planned a special weekend getaway to a bed and breakfast. I wanted to give Sara a break from everyday life, a break from the stress of her parents' divorce and our difficult marriage. The weekend away was the best time we had spent together in months, yet the divorce of Sara's parents and our own marital problems rested heavily on our backs. One night Sara and I decided that we would try to forget our problems and all of the heartache of her parents' divorce, just for a couple of hours. But it didn't work. We ended up sitting by the fireplace in the room; Sara cried and told me horrible things that had happened in her parents' marriage, things that she was telling me for the first time.

Remembering Sara's anger over my lack of sympathy, I listened intently. Wide-eyed, I nodded and tried to imagine the pain that she must be feeling. She had learned that much of her parents' marriage—much of what she knew to be true about life—was a lie.

Back to College

Sara had been working at a publishing company since we moved back from California, but she missed teaching desperately. She began looking into getting her state teaching certification, which would require going back to school and taking the education classes she never took as an undergraduate student. After looking at several schools, Sara settled on a local college where she could complete the required coursework in just under a year by taking classes full-time.

I supported Sara's decision to go back to school, but it meant we'd only have one income and would need a more conservative budget. Sara had never closed the personal bank account that she opened when we were separated, and she assured me that she would pay for her education out of that account. "It's my money," she said, as if I would have a problem with the cost.

"Sara, I don't even think we should have two bank accounts, and I'm not worried about the money it will take for you to go back to school. In fact, I'd rather we pay for this together," I said.

But I was concerned about the cost, primarily because Sara chose to attend a private school, which would cost nearly three times more than the local public university. But with all of our other problems, money was the least of my worries.

My biggest fear was that something would happen once Sara completed school. Some part of me always wondered if she might try to leave again after she had finished school. I never thought that she actually would, but on some subconscious level, I was aware of the possibility.

Small Steps

I knew that if things didn't change, I was going to lose all sense of who I was and who I could be. So I told Sara that I wasn't going to share all of my thoughts with her anymore—I emotionally couldn't cope with the burden of doing that. It wasn't that I was trying to make things difficult for her. I simply couldn't. She was irritated but said little about it other than that she didn't agree with me.

I started taking other small steps of rebellion. One day when Sara was away, I called my best friend from college, the one Sara didn't want me talking to anymore. I hardly mentioned Sara in our conversation, but I wanted to talk to him. There was nothing wrong with talking to him about things outside of our marriage, was there? And so I did. When I told Sara, she was bewildered. "Why wouldn't you ask me first? It's a pretty big deal that you did that."

I could see that she was getting nervous. She didn't like it when she wasn't in control. And she was starting to lose some control.

Chapter Ten

The Last Night and First Weeks

In my dream, I was drowning my sorrows
But my sorrows they'd learned to swim
—"Until the End of the World," U2

As the phone rang, I felt a pain in my chest.

I was on a business trip and had just returned to my hotel room. I wasn't expecting a call, especially from Sara. I had just been thinking about her, but that wasn't unusual. I was always thinking about her, worrying about her, wondering how to make her happy, wondering how to preserve my emotional health and our marriage at the same time. I was shocked to hear her voice—she rarely called when we were apart. I had called Sara nearly every day that week, but this was the first time she had called me.

Sara had expressed little interest in me for almost six months. In fact, she usually preferred not to talk to me at all. So why was she suddenly calling—and calling so late? I looked at the clock. It was almost 11:00 p.m.

"Hey," she said as I picked up the phone.

"Hey, I'm glad you called," I said. "How's it going?"

"Okay."

"Your timing is great. I just got back to my room. I was down in the lobby with Ben."

We made small talk for a few minutes. I told her about my day, told her about the convention I was attending. I was so eager to get some sort of positive response from her. But there was nothing ... and then ...

"Well ... I just called because ... I wanted you to know something," she said.

"Okay ... "

"I just wanted you to know that I really loved you," she said, almost whispering.

Loved—past tense.

"I love you, too," I said, grasping the phone as tightly as I could, pulling it as close to my mouth as possible—as if physically moving closer to Sara.

For two years people had expressed concern about Sara—friends, family, counselors, even a friend of hers. Concern about how she was controlling me, concern about how she was punishing me. But I continually tried to move closer to her.

For two years I had wrestled with the shame and depression and guilt that Sara always seemed to hold over my head. I had so many questions: Were our personality differences too great? Was she too hard on me? Did my mistakes awaken some deep wound in Sara, a wound from which she would never recover?

"You're not a good match," my counselor told me that one day. "She's emotionally abusing you," another had said to me. None of this made any sense. How could my wife be bad for me? She was the one who I had committed to "for better or for worse"—before God and friends and family. Everything was so confusing—evil and good, healthy and unhealthy, my sin and her sin. Commitment and sanity hanging in the balance, in tension with one another. Yet that night, all I could think of was how badly I wanted things to work, how badly I wanted to be the hero—to prove my worth. I wanted our marriage to be an example of how God can restore relationships.

But for our marriage, there would be no restoration.

That night in the hotel room, as I clutched the phone, there was something so unnatural about what Sara was saying and how she was saying it. It was the first time in months that she had spoken to me with gentleness, yet her words were all in the past tense—loved. I tried to convince myself that things were getting better, but deep down I knew better. Deep down I knew a storm was brewing.

Before we hung up, I couldn't ignore the fact that she was acting strangely. She kept saying things like, "I just want you to know that I've never tried to hurt you." She must have said that at least four times.

"I know you've never tried to hurt me," I said. "We've had a tough marriage, but things will get better. I love you, and I'll see you tomorrow. Wait—before you go, will you be there when I get home?"

"I don't know," she said.

"Do you have errands to run or something?" I asked.

"I don't know," she repeated.

"Okay, well, I'll be back around 11:00 tomorrow morning if you can be there. I love you."

My head was spinning. I had no idea what to make of her comments, which made me even more anxious to get home. I expected to see her the next day when I returned from my trip. But there was something forlorn, something distant in her voice. It was as if she was saying goodbye without ever truly saying goodbye.

As of that night, we had been reunited for almost two years, but our reunion had been a nightmare. She didn't even want to go to counseling anymore. We slept in the same bed, lived in the same apartment, but couldn't have been further apart.

I felt trapped. Alone. "God, You're the only one who can put this back together," I thought. That evening as I hung up the phone, I stared out the hotel window. The downtown skyline twinkled in the darkness. It was an incredible view, dozens of stories above the city, hundreds of miles from home. But I didn't feel like I was on top of the world. I felt like I was in hell.

What happened to the girl I married? What happened to the girl who laughed late into the night with me? What happened to the girl who loved everything about me?

Though I had many questions, there were two things I knew: I wasn't the spiritual giant I had convinced Sara I was. I was all too human, all too selfish, all too sinful. I also knew that Sara was far from an innocent bystander. She had problems with control and anger—problems she refused to deal with, problems that hurt our marriage.

That night in the hotel room, on the eve of my return home, I was filled with the same feeling I had as a child when tornado sirens blared at my elementary school. During those frightening times, which seemed almost apocalyptic then, everyone would huddle in a concrete shelter built into the side of a hill. We would stand shoulder to shoulder as teachers nervously scanned their grade books, putting a check next to the name of each child accounted for. During those times I remember closing my eyes and praying, "God, keep my family safe. Don't let the storm hit them." At twenty-six, scared and alone in a hotel room, I prayed that the tornado wouldn't hit me. "God, hold this marriage together. Don't let this storm hit me."

But it did. And it hit with a vengeance.

Welcome Home

When I opened the door to our apartment the next day, I was stunned. The first thing I noticed was an empty stretch of carpet where our couch had been only days earlier. I staggered over

129

to the kitchen table, where keys were neatly placed alongside a typed letter. The letter was a matter-of-fact listing of what bills had been paid, where things had been placed, and what items she took. "I left you with enough to be comfortable," she wrote. There was no explanation for her leaving. There was no new address or phone number given. All I had were two albums of wedding pictures and a shoebox with every letter I had ever written her. She decided to leave those behind.

I was devastated. My heart felt like lead.

I felt as if someone had just hit me in the stomach with a baseball bat. I was speechless. I could hardly comprehend what I was looking at. I felt as if I were at the scene of a crime, a crime the police would never investigate, a crime that was perfectly legal.

"This can't be happening," I thought to myself. "This isn't happening. I can't deal with this. I have no way to deal with this."

My entire body was shaking. I called a friend whom I had met just months earlier. There were so many people I could've called, many I knew so much better, but I called this friend. I told him what had happened, and he promised to pray right away. He also told me something startling: He had been married before. He was now remarried, but his first wife had left him. God knew how much I admired this friend. I believe God put it on my heart to call him so that I might learn this. In the midst of despair, a seed was planted: If Sara never came back, God wasn't done with me. He wouldn't give up on me, just as He hadn't given up on my friend.

I was still shaking as I called Jon, another friend and a coworker. It was almost noon, and he suggested that we meet at a nearby restaurant. Thirty minutes later we were at Applebee's. I told Jon what had happened, told him what the letter said. Wide-eyed, Jon listened, shaking his head. He had nothing to say.

Afterward, behind the wheel of my car, I realized that I had nowhere to go. Sitting in the parking lot, staring into the hazy summer day, I watched couples getting out of their cars, holding hands, laughing. I wondered how anyone could be happy on a day like this. Their happiness seemed to mock my pain. I felt like drinking poison; I felt like slipping softly into eternity. This life seemed over.

Since I had just gotten back from a business trip, I wasn't planning to go into work that day. I drove back to my apartment, hoping that Sara had left a message on the answering machine. She hadn't.

Desperate, I drove to the home of a couple who led the Bible study that Sara and I attended. Although it was the middle of the day, I knew there was a chance they would be home since they were both retired. Finding them in their front yard, I told them I needed to talk. They invited me inside. With a weak voice, I told them what happened. We prayed together, and when we were done, I felt just as sad, just as shocked.

When I got back to my apartment, I could hardly think straight. I paced back and forth, holding my phone, putting it down, turning on my computer, turning it off. I finally thought of one way I could contact Sara: email. Yes, she must still have her email address. I sent her a long email, begging her to come home, begging her to call me.

"Sara, why would you leave without telling me where I could

find you? Why are you doing this? I am so upset. I don't know what to do ..."

Though I didn't know what to do, I had to do something. I hopped in my car and began driving around the city, looking for Sara's car. "Where are you, Sara? Where are you? Please, God, help me find her." There was an apartment complex nearby, and I drove through the complex, carefully eyeing the carports, praying as I drove past each cluster of apartments that I would find Sara's car. After about fifteen minutes, I realized that trying to find Sara was nearly impossible. She could be anywhere in a metro area of more than 1 million people.

It was a humid day; my shirt stuck to my back as I returned to my apartment. I called another friend who offered to meet me for dinner. I thanked him but decided that I would head back to my parents' house instead. Throwing some clothes in a bag, I was reminded of two years earlier when Sara had kicked me out of the apartment.

This time, she let me have the apartment all to myself.

Paper Trail

I dreaded returning to my empty apartment, to the typed letter that was still on the table, to the place where the couch once was. But I had to go back to work whether I wanted to or not.

Three weeks later, a man knocked on my door holding divorce papers. For the first time since my wife left, I was furious. "How dare she do this to me," I thought. I made plenty of mistakes, but I never did anything to warrant this. She's ruined my life.

I was stunned. In legal jargon, I was being sued by Sara. It cited the all-too-common complaint of "irreconcilable differences." I contested the divorce, but in the long run it was inevitable. My father, an attorney, told me there was virtually nothing I could do. Since the only way to contact Sara was through email, I emailed often—trying to convince her to talk things through with me, asking her to pray about things, telling her why I thought she was wrong. But my impassioned pleas were met with indifferent silence.

I even enlisted people from church to try to contact her.

Nothing.

One day, I received a letter in the mail from a furniture company. It was sent to inform Sara that they had changed the mailing address on her credit card bill. It listed her new address. I just stared at the address, trying to picture in my head exactly how to get there.

I told my parents about the letter. I told them that I was tempted to go and find Sara. They told me not to go. I took their advice ... for about a week. And then after a particularly bad day at work, I decided that I had to find her. I had to tell her how I felt, and I convinced myself that if I just went once, I would get the need to see her out of my system.

Sara had moved to an apartment just twenty minutes from where I lived. It was a late summer evening as I drove with my window down, slowing my car as I found the street that led to her apartment. I found her apartment number and parked my car. Walking toward the front door, I looked for her car but didn't see it. There were garages along the periphery of the parking lot, and I wondered if her car was in one of those, hidden from view.

None of the apartments were accessible from the outside. There was one front door through which everyone entered. As I stood at that front door, I saw the last names of those who lived in that particular building.

Despite the warm summer temperatures, a chill went up my spine when I caught the name: "Conant."

That was the only thing that I would eventually ask for in the divorce—that she change her last name. How dare she leave and then try to keep my name! If she hated me so much, why would she want to do this? Perhaps she didn't want to, perhaps it was only a matter of time before she legally changed it herself. But I asked, just in case.

As I stood at the entrance to the apartment building, I wondered if she was in there. I wondered if she would answer. I breathed deeply and pressed the button. I heard a buzzing noise, but no one answered. I pressed it again and again. Still no answer. I stood there, pressing the button repeatedly. Nothing. Finally I walked around to the back of the apartment building where some of the porches overlooked a small common area.

I saw one of our green-striped beach chairs on a third-floor balcony. We had received two beach chairs for our wedding. Sara left one for me and took the other. That was the closest I got to Sara that night, and perhaps ever again. Perhaps I should have never gone searching for Sara, but I was right about one thing: I did get it out of my system. I would never again return. I would never again search for Sara.

A Bad Christian

I was left with smashed pieces of myself, wondering how they could ever be glued back together again. I thought, "How will

I ever get through this?" So much of me was a part of her and perhaps always would be. But more and more, I began to think about how others would view me: Will they think I'm a "bad" Christian because I'm divorced? What if I didn't want the divorce—does that make me okay? What will people think that I did? What if they get the wrong impression?

I didn't know to explain to friends, family, and coworkers what had happened.

One day a coworker who attends my church said, "I remember when I met your wife on the women's retreat ..."

"My wife left and filed for divorce," I quickly said.

She looked shocked. I'm sure this coworker pictured Sara and me as the perfect couple. She thought of us as two smiling faces straight out of a J.Crew catalog—well dressed, young, happy, and seemingly perfect. In fact, people routinely commented on how we looked like the "perfect" couple. How little they knew. How deceiving appearances are.

Shortly after Sara left, I decided to tell several colleagues in my department that Sara had left. We were in a staff meeting—six of us in the room—and at the end of the meeting I said, "I'd like to tell everyone something. Two weeks ago, my wife unexpectedly left and filed for divorce. I just wanted to let you know. Needless to say, it's been really tough." My face was red with embarrassment. I felt like I might cry. But I knew that I had to tell them, and the easiest way was to tell them all at once.

Word spread to other departments. One day another coworker who I didn't know very well came by my office. He wanted to offer his condolences, but he didn't know what to say. "I heard about your situation—what's happening," he said. "I just want you to know that ... I know ... I know it's really hard."

Each day, I felt so self-conscious about my divorce. I remember thinking, "If I ever date again, no one normal will ever like me. No one normal will ever go out with me. Who would be interested in someone like me—someone who's divorced?"

I felt like damaged goods—perhaps even more so because of the crazy notion that "real" Christians don't get divorced. But sometimes I wonder if "real" Christians aren't actually those people who have the guts to admit that they're not where they want to be, who have the courage to admit they still haven't found what they're looking for. I wonder if real Christians aren't the ones who realize that all of us—from the best of us to the worst of us—have dark places, dark memories, and dark nights of the soul.

As the weeks and months passed, I began to realize that the important questions don't revolve around what people think about me. The important questions revolve around Jesus: Am I seeking and pursuing Jesus? How am I letting my pain make me more like Jesus? How can I use my experience to help others? What is God calling me to do in light of my divorce? Have I forgiven my wife as Jesus asks? Have I forgiven myself?

There were no easy answers to these questions. And it seemed as if there were no easy answers to anything anymore.

Chapter Eleven

Death

The heart that hurts
Is a heart that beats

—"One Step Closer," U2

I enjoy visiting cemeteries. It's a strange hobby, I realize. It's not something I do often, but when I'm near one, I enjoy walking around, wondering what these people's lives were like: Who did they love? Who loved them? Did they accomplish what they hoped to accomplish in life? What were their last thoughts before they died?

I especially enjoy visiting the oldest graves. Sometimes I'll crouch down and read the chipped engravings. "What year was that? What was their name?" I carefully wipe away the dirt on the engraved lettering. I think about the day the person died.

I wonder what the relatives said, I wonder what friends whispered in quiet moments, I wonder who was never the same afterward ... I wonder.

And I always wonder if anyone ever visits these old places. Some of the graves memorialize people who died so long ago that they've been completely forgotten by everyone. Even the people who loved them are now dead. No one visits; no one brings flowers or flags or remembers the important dates in these people's lives. Generations later, it's as if they had never lived.

I remember at least two occasions when my wife and I spent time in cemeteries together. One of those times was a few months before Sara left. The day was overcast and cold—the kind of day when you stuff your hands deep into your pockets and your shoulder muscles tense involuntarily.

On this day we drove down narrow cemetery roads together, talking about death. I asked Sara whether she would want to be buried or cremated. The question hung in the air. I could tell that she didn't want to answer. But when I asked the question, I remember thinking that I should listen carefully: What if Sara dies before I do?

My perspective has changed drastically since then. If she died today, would I even be invited to the funeral? Even if she died, would that be the official end to our relationship? Our relationship seems to go on and on, no matter what I do. Our souls seem forever entangled despite the months that pass, despite the changes in our lives.

She is still a part of me, and I am part of her.

A friend of mine who has been divorced said, "I don't think you ever really get over it." We wondered why that was; we wondered why the world reacts so differently when someone physically dies. When someone dies, friends and family bring casseroles; they travel from afar to attend funeral services. They send cards and notes of encouragement and make phone calls. They join you at the cemetery and mourn. Their very presence brings healing.

So why is it that when a marriage dies, people do nothing?

When my marriage died, I was left on a ledge with little to no support. Friends and family didn't know what to say, so they often said nothing. No one visited; no one sent cards.

But when someone dies, there is comfort for those who feel the loss. There is a tangible, physical reminder of the loss. There is a body. There is a tombstone. There are ashes, rituals, prayers, community. It's obvious that I will never get these things; it's obvious I will never have the same comfort that widows receive.

But what about community? What about the group of people who sat at my wedding—the people who agreed to support my marriage? Where are they now? I still see their faces, smiling and laughing. I see them with glasses of champagne. I see them handing me wrapped gifts—pots and pans, pillows, other things that are now shoved to the back of cupboards and closets. Things that I would gladly trade for a hug or a phone call.

Today, these wedding guests are only a memory. Today, they are like passengers on the *Titanic*, celebrating while a disaster that they know nothing about is on its way. I wish my wedding guests were around to support my marriage, but communities have become fragmented. The people who attended my wedding live in dozens of cities around the country, and most of them never knew there were problems in my marriage until they heard about my divorce.

Most of them probably know now, but what should they say? What should they do? I don't know. They don't know.

And so I am relegated to the old parts of cemeteries—the parts no one remembers, the parts no one cares about. The parts no one visits, the parts no one acknowledges.

Perhaps I might feel more peace—more finality—if there were a gravestone marking the death of my relationship with Sara. But all that marks the end of our marriage is sad memories. There is nothing tangible, nothing that I can kneel by and mourn over.

What if I created a gravestone? What if I really did it? What would it say? Maybe this: "Here in this place we put to rest our pain, our sadness, our happiness, our love; we mark it as dead. Here in this place we kneel and cry. Here we have a monument to our relationship. And that is all that we have."

I wish I could end this discussion on a more positive note, but I'm not sure I can because graveyards—whether they are physical or emotional graveyards—are places where things end, dead places. However, graveyards were never the end for Jesus.

Jesus cried one day after learning that a friend had died. Filled with emotion, Jesus walked to the graveyard, stood in front of the tomb, and said, "Come out." And the dead man came out. The greatest graveyard miracle of all happened three days after officials proclaimed Jesus dead—His followers found His tomb empty. They soon learned that Jesus had begun His new life— His eternal life. Jesus created new life out of dead things.

As sad as graveyards seem, sometimes they're not the end; sometimes they're the beginning of something else. So as I bury my marriage, what will Jesus do? Can something be reborn in this dead place? To be honest, I am so cynical and sad that I wonder if such a miracle is possible. What will come out of my personal graveyard?

Hopefully something that looks less like me and more like Jesus. Hopefully something that resembles a miracle.

Ignoring Our Death

I spent the first Thanksgiving after my divorce at my parents' house. It felt strange. There was so much that I couldn't share, so many things left unsaid. My divorce was rarely spoken of, but we were all aware of it. Sympathetic smiles at dinner, hugs that tried to convey words that aunts and uncles and cousins wanted to say but couldn't.

After dinner, we watched a film of my mother from almost fifty years ago. As I stood there watching the silent film, I realized how alone I was, how alone we all are.

In the film, my grandmother—the perfect 1950s housewife— tends to her children. She's wearing starched dresses and stylish jewelry, supervising birthday parties where all the right games are played in all the right ways. My mom—a beautiful little girl, brown hair curled at the ends—plays musical chairs with neighborhood children; it's a birthday party fit for an avocado-green suburban childhood.

My grandmother did everything right, from planning parties to instilling her children with the best of manners. But years after the children were raised—babies' butts wiped countless times, money saved, groceries bought, and meals cooked for years on end—my grandfather left. This seemingly perfect home—all the best appliances, the children dressed in all the right clothes—crumbled in an instant.

I don't sit in judgment of my grandfather. I don't know why he left. But I see how divorce has shaped my grandmother's life. Today, when her hip is hurting, she has no one to help her. Today, when she'd love to talk to someone, her dog and her television keep her company.

I saw the distant look in her eyes as the old Technicolor-style film rolled. She should be watching this on the couch with my grandfather, holding his hand, wistfully looking into his eyes, telling him that despite the hard times, she'd marry him all over again.

But my grandfather lives hundreds of miles away, and today he spends most of his time connected to an oxygen machine. He remarried a long time ago, but I wonder if he ever thinks of my grandmother; I wonder if he ever regrets leaving. I wonder what he would say, how he would feel if he sat and watched the film I watched that day.

How much does a single life affect another single life? Ask my grandmother. Ask my mom. Ask her three brothers. All of them have private pains, private hurts that will never fully heal.

I wished Sara could've seen me hug my grandmother goodbye. Grandma had trouble zipping her coat, so I helped her. And as

I hugged her goodbye, she said, "I'm tired." And she was. Not just physically tired, but emotionally tired. Tired of being alone. Tired of her grandchildren playing video games and surfing the Internet when she wanted nothing more than to have someone sit next to her and ask her about life, about anything.

I hugged her for a long time and said nothing. But I wanted to say, "I know, Grandma. I know you're tired. I'm tired, too. I'm really tired."

I suppose that in some ways Thanksgiving was as happy as it could be. For as much as I wanted to bare my soul to my family, to tell them about my divorce, I'm not sure they really wanted to hear about it. We're all so self-absorbed.

I wish I could just do a better job loving my family, helping my family instead of looking for their sympathy. They have just as many dead places as I do—places that I know nothing about. And if I took the time to get to know them, maybe I would find that they are just as tired as Grandma, just as tired as I am.

Praying Our Death

We read Psalm 90 the other night in Bible study, which author Eugene Peterson calls "Praying Our Death" in The Message. It's an appropriate name, for we learn that death and pain are inescapable: "All we can remember is that frown on your face. Is that all we're ever going to get? We live for seventy years or so (with luck we might make it to eighty), and what do we have to show for it? Trouble. Toil and trouble and a marker in the graveyard" (Ps. 90: 9–10, MSG).

This entire psalm speaks of pain and death as natural parts of life, parts of the cycle of nature that are as inevitable as the changing of seasons. So why do we act so offended when some-one dies or when something bad happens to us?

Someone in my Bible study group noted that it's interesting how we try so hard to "let God off the hook" by writing books that explain "why bad things happen to good people."

Yet this psalm seems to indicate that bad things happen all the time—and the psalmist doesn't try to defend any of us as "good," either: "You have set our iniquities before you, our secret sins in the light of your presence" (Ps. 90:8).

I don't mean to imply that all evil is ordered by God specifically to punish us. But it's an interesting—and not very modern—notion to think of evil and death as something we deserve by the very fact that we are all sinful. "All our days pass away under your wrath," the psalmist writes.

It's strange to think of how life must have been thousands of years ago when this psalm was written—when death and pain weren't obscured by modern hospitals and sterile waiting rooms, when people weren't kept alive on respirators or healed by miracle surgeries and wonder drugs.

People didn't die miles away in a hospital on the edge of town. They died at home, and people wailed and cried and ripped their clothes for all to see. They mourned publicly, not quietly in the catacombs of a modern hospital.

In our Bible study, we talked about deaths that we have mourn-ed. We talked about deaths that have killed parts of us.

I thought immediately of a pastor I knew—Bob Gaddini—who

always called me "bro." He was the type of guy that everyone loved—he had two beautiful children and a beautiful wife, and he was always laughing and smiling and playing pranks. He was in his forties when one morning he was hit by a car during a bike ride. The driver didn't stop to help, and Bob was found on the side of the road dead some time later. To my knowledge, they never found the driver who hit him.

One woman talked about the death of her brother. He was only nineteen when he got in the car early one morning with their mother. They were picking up their father, a railroad man who worked several hours away. On the way there as the boy slept in the front seat—glasses on, head against the window—a drunk driver slammed his car into the door that the boy leaned against. The boy died in his mother's arms. Later, her mother said that as her son gasped for his final breaths, she was transported nineteen years back in time, holding him as a newborn as he struggled for his first breaths.

I didn't tell my story, but I could have. Of course, you know it by now. The death of my marriage, the day I was left gasping for breath, the day I realized that if you pray enough and try hard enough and become "spiritual" enough, you still may not get what you want—or even what you think God wants.

I guess Psalm 90 makes sense to me. I feel as if I have lived it.

Yet the psalmist leaves us with a cry of hope. One of the last verses reads: "Make us glad for as many days as you have afflict-ed us, for as many years as we have seen trouble ..." (Ps. 90:15).

Yes, God. Make us glad for as many days as you have afflicted us, for as many years as we have seen trouble. Make us glad on this planet of tears.

145

Remembering Our Death

Lent is my favorite season of the church calendar because it reminds me of an important reality: Living the "Jesus Life" is not easy.

The Jesus Life is not the happy-go-lucky "Jesus is my home-boy" life that pop culture would have us believe. The Jesus Life is not the health, wealth, and prosperity life that television evangelists would have us believe. The Jesus Life is not the politically driven "us versus them" life that some Christian leaders would have us believe.

The Jesus Life was best expressed on a crude wooden cross: Nails. Blood. Death. Love. Forgiveness. Sacrifice. The Jesus Life is about going out into the world and taking up our cross as Jesus did and as He commanded us to do.

During Lent, we remember the sufferings that Jesus endured. We remember His final days on earth and ultimately His passion for the world, which is most beautifully expressed in the Stations of the Cross.

The stations are practiced not only by Catholic Christians, but increasingly by many Protestant Christians as well. The stations take us through the entire story of Jesus' final hours, from His being condemned to death on a cross to His rising from the dead.

As we walk the stations, praying and meditating on these various scenes from Jesus' final hours, we remember that "by his wounds we are healed" (Isa. 53:5). And strangely, though there are so many places that are sick inside of me, I can attest to the reality of being healed by the wounds of Jesus.

When I meditate on the wounds of Jesus, several things seem to happen: the cancer of self-centeredness is removed, the sadness fades, the pain becomes bearable, the ordinary becomes holy, gratitude increases, healing takes place. But because I am human, I will become sick again soon, and I will need to again return to the cross, to the scourging, to the sacrifice.

But even more than a prayerful, meditative exercise, Lent has become part of my history. In some small way, I now identify with Jesus as He cries from the cross, "My God, my God, why have you forsaken me?" (Matt. 27:46).

I now see that I too am called to take up my cross, to become humble to death, to love my enemies as Jesus did when He said of His torturers, "Father, forgive them for they do not know what they are doing" (Luke 23:34).

Two years ago, I realized that my marriage was the cross I was called to carry, and my wife the enemy I was called to love. And by understanding this, I knew that I could endure whatever pain my marriage caused; I knew I could endure whether my relationship with my wife improved or not. I saw that pain was beautiful because I was in some sense participating in the sufferings of Jesus.

I was not only meditating on the Stations of the Cross, I was experiencing them in my own life in some mysterious way.

I suppose since Sara left, Lent has become even more important to me. I am even more aware of my need for Jesus, my need for His sacrifice, my need for His mercy.

Accepting Our Death

The other day I learned that a well-known marriage seminar was coming to town. "Learn God's plan for marriage," the promotional video proclaimed during the 11:00 a.m. church service. I sat in my seat, arms folded, cynically looking at the video screen. "What plan for marriage?" I thought to myself.

My wife and I had been to this particular marriage conference before, and nothing had come of it except more pain and hurt and frustration. Despite my problems with the conference, I think that it has done a tremendous amount of good for many couples. So why didn't I experience God's plan for marriage? Maybe it's because there's something wrong with "God's plan for marriage"—us. We're the problem.

We're selfish and sinful and unwilling to forgive, unwilling to live out the command of Jesus to turn the other cheek, unwilling to take a punch in the face and come back with a kiss. It's a hard thing to do, even for those of us who really want to love and follow Jesus.

There's another problem with "God's plan for marriage." There isn't a plan. Yes, there are commands and stories and teachings in Scripture that express God's desire for marriage. But a "plan"? No. Perhaps I'm splitting hairs, but I wonder if using this kind of language implies that having a great marriage is as simple as looking at a map or following a recipe. Take a left turn on State Street and then a right at the third stoplight and you're there! Start with some flour, add a little oil, some butter, salt, and cook at 350 degrees for twenty minutes, and voila! Flaky, buttery crust with minimal effort! Marriage is not the same as baking quiche.

I can't handle easy answers to difficult situations anymore, which is why I sometimes cringe at well-intentioned statements like "God's plan for marriage." And I'm noticing more and more that others feel the same way. Friends. Musicians. Poets. In the U2 song "City of Blinding Lights," Bono sings, "The more you see, the less you know, the less you find out as you go. I knew much more then than I do now."

I know much less now than I did when I got married—even after attending Christian conferences and reading dozens of Christian books. In fact, I can remember life as a senior in college: confident in my politics, outwardly confident in my faith, sure of myself and my abilities, self-assured that Sara and I had tackled every obstacle in our relationship, certain that all that awaited us was a life of wonderful sex and exciting adventures.

But like Bono, I must admit that I knew (or thought I knew) much more then than I do now. Now I realize that my politics don't always work or make things better; in fact, sometimes they're just plain wrong. I now realize that marriage is a mystery, not a paint-by-numbers way to sexual and emotional satisfaction. And now I realize that faith is the ultimate mystery—a journey with fits and starts, a journey with more lows than highs, a journey that never ends, even when we're ready for it to be over.

Standing above all of my problems—our problems—high above a world of self-indulgence and pain is not a president or a top military leader, but a humble rabbi from the Middle East named Jesus. God in the flesh. Emmanuel. God with us. He is so much greater than us, and His ways are so much higher than our ways. Yet He was one of us. He walked among us. And He loved unlike anyone has ever loved before or since—even those of us who never figured out His plan for marriage.

Speaking Our Death

I recently sat with a friend as she ate dinner. Unexpectedly, she began talking about the difficulties that she and her husband have faced, from having a child too young to a period of separation that they endured. In some ways her story resembled mine, and I hurt for her and her husband. She talked about how upset her husband was when they were separated, how he cried and pleaded, how she took him back.

She talked about not knowing if she loved him anymore, how she felt more like a mother to her husband than a wife. Today she wonders if she should simply end their relationship, if it's worth it—if they are really meant for each other, or if they are simply living out the consequences of having sex too young.

She wonders if she will regret staying with him.

"I just don't know if we're going to make it," she said matter-of-factly. "I mean, I'm still young—I still have my entire life ahead of me. I really care about him; I just don't know if I love him."

I noticed that as she talked about leaving her husband, she might as well have been talking about what to eat for breakfast the next day. Her disposition was cold, detached. She was mentally and emotionally exhausted, as if she had all but resigned herself to the fact that their relationship would soon die, or that it had already died and she was the only person who had noticed.

"He doesn't even talk about how he feels about things," she said. "We were separated, and then before I knew it, we were back together again, and we never really even talked about what happened."

I couldn't help but try to encourage her to work things out with her husband, to get to the bottom of what might be making her feel this way, to understand why her husband has difficulty sharing his emotions.

I tried to explain how so often I pointed the finger at my ex-wife, when in many cases I was the problem.

"I have learned that no matter what others do to me, no matter how many people I run from, I can't run from myself," I said. "I bring my own faults and bad habits and selfishness into any relationship. I can look around and imagine what another woman might be like—how wonderful she might be, how kind, how loving—when in fact, if I knew her, I mean really knew her, I probably wouldn't like her nearly as much as I imagine that I might, because I would find that unfortunately she is human, just like me."

I told my friend a story that illustrated my point. I once went to see a well-known musician play. Between songs a fan yelled, "I love you!" And this famous music artist paused and quizzically said, "That's because you don't know me." It was a profound statement from a man who has been through divorce, who has struggled with drugs, and who, according to one interview that I read, wonders if the universe really cares about him or anyone else. It was the sort of statement that I was trying to get my friend to understand and accept.

But before I could elaborate on the point and climb back up on my soapbox, this friend asked me if I was better off as a result of my divorce.

"Better off? Well, I've lost a part of myself. Part of me has died. I will never be the same, and I will always have to deal with that. But I guess I am happier in some ways, I suppose I'm more at peace with my own faults and imperfections now."

In hindsight, I realize that the best way I could have described to my friend how I really felt about my divorce was to have told her this: The one person I feel like I need to talk to is the one person I never will.

Chapter Twelve

Wrestling with God and Demons

I have spoke with the tongue of angels
I have held the hand of a devil
It was warm in the night
I was cold as a stone
—"I Still Haven't Found What I'm Looking For," U2

I didn't want to wake up, but my ceiling was shaking. It was my upstairs neighbor's stereo. I threw off my covers and walked into the kitchen, squinting. As sun poured through the windows, I felt guilty.

It was Sunday.

"I should've made it to the 11:00 a.m. service," I told myself.

But what good was church, anyway? I never really liked church. Too often, people smiled when they didn't want to, gossiped under the guise of "prayer requests," and railed against immorality while practicing their own brand of it when no one was looking. I should know—in some ways, I was once one of them.

My church did much to contradict these negative stereotypes, but I still felt disconnected, especially when I started going to church alone. The people at my church only knew me as married. The same was true for those who attended a Bible study that my wife and I had joined only six months earlier. Now it was just me.

The leader of the Bible study was in his seventies. He invented the Pop-Tart—that tasty, sugar-glazed treat you put in the toaster. Now retired, he spent his time speaking, carving wood, and shooting squirrels with a pellet gun.

Another member, in his forties, held a PhD from Boston College. An editor by trade, he had the sensibilities of a philosopher. He usually said something you wanted to write down. His wife was a pastor and a chaplain—not to mention an intellectual in her own right. They sometimes read from Bible versions I had never heard of.

There were two others in the group as well—an insurance agent and a social worker.

I was the only one in my twenties, which was sometimes difficult. I was from a different generation entirely—one familiar with MTV and video games, not Woodstock or World War II. I sometimes felt isolated and strange.

I stayed with this eclectic group, even though it wasn't easy, especially when someone would ask God to "bless" my ex-wife. I thought, "No! Don't bless her! Why are you saying that? How stupid can you be—do you have any idea what I'm going through?"

Back at church, I felt just as vulnerable, and sometimes just as angry. I felt all eyes watching me—watching me slink into my seat ten minutes late, watching me run out of church immediately after the closing prayer. I was always terrified that someone might ask, "Where's your wife?"

Church felt like high school all over again. I felt like a teenager being dropped off by my parents in front of school. The cool kids—the ones with their own cars—would watch as I climbed out of my father's minivan. In their eyes, I was a loser. A failure. I felt the same way at church. Married people would watch me walk through the glass doors—shoulders slumped, sad, alone. I was a loser again. I was divorced.

The fact that I was now divorced became especially apparent at church, where everyone wore nametags. There was a bulletin board with everyone's nametag, including Sara's. I never looked for it, but I knew it was there. It was like a nagging pain that never went away, a reminder that life would never be the same.

I never had the courage to remove her nametag—that seemed too painful—so I asked a friend to do it. One day he told me that he had thrown it away.

Unfortunately, it didn't produce the effect I thought it would. Her presence was still in that church, looming over the sanctuary, walking through the hallways, singing in the choir. She will always be in that church. But I knew the solution wasn't to go somewhere else. She would just follow me.

After Sara left, I did a lot of thinking about church: its purpose, its role in my life, its shortcomings. And my conclusion could be summarized in three words: Church of Losers. That's where I wanted to go to church.

Why? Because I'm tired of everyone acting like they have it all together, tired of illusions that we have perfect lives, perfect families. I'm also tired of myself, tired of my reticence to open up and bare my soul, tired of avoiding people, tired of my unwillingness to get involved in the ministry of the church.

I'm tired of the notion that I'm screwed up ... "But don't worry, we have a support group for people like you!" But, by its very name, the Church of Losers says: Come here if you're a loser—we're all losers!

Everyone at my church is a mess—I'm a mess—so why can't we admit it? Why do we spend so much time trying to convince each other that we're not?

Why do we ask our friends to throw away painful memories? Instead, why don't we say: "Here's the nametag that my wife once wore—she doesn't go here anymore because she filed for divorce and never wants to see me again. You probably don't understand how hard it is for me to throw this away! Please pray for me. I feel like hell. I need Jesus so badly, but I have such a hard time finding Him. Will someone here be Jesus for me today?"

Numbing Medicine

As I stood in my kitchen on that church-less Sunday morning, I felt a headache coming. I grabbed a bottle of Excedrin and swallowed two pills, chasing them with Gatorade. I then noticed that for the third day in a row, I felt a pain in my chest. I attributed it to the extreme amount of stress I was under—the type of stress I haven't felt since I was a freshman in college.

I wondered if writing this book was triggering my pain. In writing, I have relived the stress, the sadness, and the anxiety of my marriage.

I grabbed a bottle of liquid antacid and measured four teaspoons over the sink. Sipping the teal-colored medicine, I began to think about the previous night.

The casual observer would have called it a date, though we didn't. We called ourselves friends. We had dinner at an expensive restaurant and then rented a movie. As we watched the movie, legs touching, all sorts of thoughts went through my head, but two in particular: She's beautiful. I'm lonely.

I also thought about the fact that it had been less than six months since my wife left. Divorced and incredibly vulnerable, I realized that I would do almost anything to ease my pain. And one way to do that would be to press my lips against hers. It would be so easy, and I would feel so much better ... at least for a moment.

But annoying thoughts kept stopping me: thoughts about Jesus, thoughts about my motives, thoughts about this woman and how she (or I) might feel if our relationship was short lived.

As I got into my car that night, I wondered if she was the right one for me or just someone for me. I didn't know. My judgment was clouded because I still had so much pain to work through—pain that only I could face.

How badly I wanted a companion, how badly I wanted to work through that pain with her, how badly I wanted my bitter cup taken from me.

I now realize that Jesus felt these same emotions. He was tempted to take the easy road over the one that led to death. The Scriptures say that Jesus prayed, "My father, if it is possible, may this cup be taken from me. Yet not as I will, but as you will" (Matt. 26:39).

If Jesus wanted to avoid pain, shouldn't I expect to feel the same impulse? Yet look at how He handled it: "Not as I will, but as you will."

Almost everything inside me wants to reject that statement. "No, God, I deserve some pleasure. I don't care if that's Your plan or not. I'm interested in what I want. I've gone through enough pain. I'm done waiting for things to get better."

Part of me wants to reject all responsibility—to deny that I'm a child of God, to deny that He's got something better for me. I want to do whatever I feel like doing at the moment.

I want to play in the sewer, usually because the sewer is all that I can see. I'm not God; I'm a human with bad vision. I can't see the ocean on the other side of my sewer.

I want to be loved by someone, even if it's a false love. I want someone to make me feel good, to believe in me.

And that night I wanted this woman. I wanted her physically and emotionally. I wanted her to help me deny who I really was. I wanted her to take away the sadness. I wanted her to be my savior.

Like me, Jesus struggled with loneliness. He wanted companionship as He faced His dark night of the soul; He needed support as He prepared to face His own death. He took three disciples with Him, telling them, "My soul is overwhelmed with sorrow to the point of death. Stay here and keep watch with me" (Matt. 26:38).

But the disciples were no help to Jesus—they kept falling asleep.

I often feel the same way. Friends don't know how to help me, so they do nothing. They fall asleep. They forget that past the calm demeanor, a storm rages inside me. Others, like the woman I watched the movie with, see the storm, but only glimpses of it. I don't know if I can trust them. I don't know if they will help me grow closer to Jesus. I don't know if I will get emotionally entangled with them only to be shoved down into the dirt, more bruised than I was before.

So, like Jesus, I invite companionship and seek community, need community—but all I really have is God. People are too much like ... people; they're too much like me. I need someone who loves in ways that I never could. I need God.

But, like Jesus, I wrestle with God. "Take this cup from me. There must be another way." And then I learn that there isn't another way. I learn that God is unreasonable. In fact, He always has been. Forgiveness is unreasonable. Jesus dying on a cross is unreasonable. A book produced from the trash heap of my life is unreasonable.

Maybe I should stop trying to understand. Perhaps, like Jesus, I should start sacrificing my will in order to find God's will. Maybe then I will see that no matter what group of believers I join on Sunday, I am already a member of the Church of Losers. All of us who follow Jesus are part of a bizarre counterculture that says, "Whoever wants to save his life will lose it, but whoever loses his life for me will find it" (Matt. 16:25).

I want to leave the sewer behind and head for the ocean. I can't see it, but if I keep walking, I think I'll find it. One thing I know for sure: I can't stay here.

Sometimes You Can't Make It on Your Own

Recently I was on a plane, thousands of feet in the air, thinking about Sara. Missing her. Earlier in the day, sitting in a deserted airport terminal in Nashville, I thought of her as I listened to the U2 song "Sometimes You Can't Make It on Your Own." Bono wrote the song about the death of his father. But the words ripped my heart open, reminding me of my relationship with Sara. They took me back to a sad, dark place inside my soul, and the effects have lasted for several days.

On the plane, I listened to these lyrics over and over again:

> It's you when I look in the mirror
> And it's you that makes it hard to let go
> Sometimes you can't make it on your own
> Sometimes you can't make it
> The best you can do is to fake it
> Sometimes you can't make it on your own

I wonder how well I'm faking it, because that's what I'm doing. Some people know me as a person who tells jokes and does silly impressions. This is certainly part of my personality, but sometimes making others laugh is my way of faking it, my way of forgetting. Forgetting that I'm emotionally devastated, forgetting that I'm on the outside looking in, forgetting that I can't make it on my own.

I Don't Belong Here

Since my divorce, I have been spending time with a group of friends who are younger than I am. Most of them are twenty-three, and I'm twenty-seven. But often I feel alienated from them. Some of them have repeatedly made comments about how I'm older or from "another generation." It seems silly to be irritated by these comments, but I am. Perhaps I'm irritated because they are truer than I'm willing to admit. In some ways, I feel like I'm closer to fifty than twenty-three.

Though I still look very young, my hair has slowly started turning gray. For a while, I tried picking out the gray hairs with tweezers. I would stand in front of the bathroom mirror, head cocked for minutes at a time, trying to pluck a single gray hair. But then I'd find another. And another. And another. I've stopped trying to do anything about it.

I want people to love me for who I am—gray haired or brown haired—not pointing out how I'm not like them. I want to be part of a community that's as natural as breathing—a community that feels effortless, comfortable, life-giving. Like being home, a place where you can put your feet on the coffee table, fix yourself something to eat, and not worry about your manners.

I want to be part of a community that is filled with grace—the kind of grace that Jesus showered on almost everyone He encountered. The people who hung around Jesus felt totally accepted and loved, no matter what their background was, no matter what they had done. Virtually anyone who had any contact with Jesus—with the exception of the religious hypo-crites—seemed to feel completely at ease with Him.

So often, I don't feel at ease around anyone.

On the weekends, I sit and think about my friends who are married. I don't want to bother them with a phone call or an unexpected visit. I feel the barrenness of my apartment: white walls, one small love seat, a couple of bookshelves, the same bed that my wife and I bought. I look up at the wreath that hangs above where our couch once was. My wife took the couch, but the wreath remains. My mom has continually tried to get me to buy more furniture.

But my sadness is bigger than a few home improvements.

My sadness extends beyond my body, beyond my soul; it extends into eternity. Life is not what I thought it was. I want to climb out of myself—"shuffle off this mortal coil," as Hamlet said. I want to rip the wreath off the wall and burn it. I want to throw my wedding ring into the ocean.

I want to renounce the faith—to say that I'm done with prayer, done with the Bible, and especially done with church. I want to scream that I'm done trying to be perfect. I want to revel in my imperfections, point them out to people, do anything but hide them.

I want to pierce myself—my ears, my nose, anything. I want to tattoo my body. I want to show people that I'm marked, cursed, dead. I want to descend into nothingness. I want to be every-thing I'm not supposed to be. I want to run from my pain, from my job, from my friends, from my past, from my life. I want to drink liquor until I feel completely numb.

But as much as I want to destroy myself and give up on faith, there's something that stops me: Jesus.

I love Jesus.

Not the blonde-haired Jesus from Sunday school. Not "political Jesus" who blesses one political party and curses another. Not the frightening Jesus who is announced through megaphones by wild-eyed fundamentalists.

I love the Jesus of the Scriptures. The Jesus who always leaves you scratching your head. The Jesus who always served other people. The Jesus who preached love above all. The Jesus who claimed to be one with the Father.

I love the Jesus who was a Jewish rabbi. The Jesus who was called a "friend of sinners." The Jesus who was rejected by the religious establishment of His day. The Jesus who said, "Come to me all you who are weary and burdened, and I will give you rest ... For my yoke is easy and my burden is light" (Matt. 11:28-30). I love the Jesus who asked us to do hard things, like take up our cross and follow Him.

I also love the story that Jesus told about the great banquet. In this story, a man prepared a great feast for a house full of guests, but when the meal was ready, people started to make excuses about why they couldn't come. One person had just purchased some property and had to go and see it. Another had just bought some oxen and was on the way to try them out. Still another had just gotten married and refused to come. So the master tells his servant, "Go out quickly into the streets and alleys of the town and bring in the poor, the crippled, the blind and the lame" (Luke 14:21). After these people fill the room, there are still more places at the table, so the master tells his servant, "Go out to the roads and country lanes and make them come in, so that my house will be full" (Luke 14:23).

I guess what stops me from losing it, what stops me from abandoning everything I know is the feeling that Jesus is asking me to come in and eat at His banquet. In my own way, I am poor and crippled and blind and lame. And if Jesus is calling me to sit at His table and eat, maybe I do belong, maybe I do have my own place, my own identity, my own house where I can put my feet up and get myself something to eat and not worry about my table manners. Maybe this is where I belong.

Jesus in the Flesh

Shortly after I began following Jesus, I had a simple insight: I would never see Jesus on this earth. I was stunned. The fact that I would never physically see the person that I love seemed almost incomprehensible. I was also stunned that a seemingly simple observation could be so earth-shaking.

Like Thomas, the disciple who doubted the resurrection of Jesus, I wanted to feel the hands of Jesus, wanted to feel the holes where the Roman soldiers drove the spikes as they crucified Him. I remember praying as I drifted to sleep that Jesus would show up in a vision, that the light of His face would surround me, that I would know—really know—that Jesus was alive.

But despite my prayers, Jesus never appeared out of thin air. No miracle for me—just disappointment, just an ordinary life with no great story to tell.

It was difficult to accept that I would never walk with a physical Jesus, never talk with a physical Jesus, never see a physical Jesus—at least on this earth.

But years later, I learned that I was wrong.

I first saw Jesus on Thanksgiving Day. I was serving lunch with Sara at a homeless shelter in Los Angeles. The funny thing was that Jesus didn't look like I thought He would. He didn't have long, wavy hair and a neatly trimmed beard. He wasn't wearing a white robe and sandals.

Standing on a street corner outside of the Fred Jordan Mission, Jesus was a middle-aged woman. Jesus looked like thousands of forty-year-old, middle-class women I had seen before—women who drove minivans and picked their kids up from soccer practice.

Holding a homeless man, Jesus was tough to miss. This man looked too dirty to touch, but this ordinary-looking Jesus—neatly dressed—had her arms wrapped around him. This Jesus—in the disguise of a middle-aged woman—wept for the homeless man. The man looked out of his mind—drunk, half-awake, brain-dead, stooped over. His face and clothes were covered in dirt and mud. He stunk. And this woman held him, mourned for him, loved him.

That is how I must look to others. I'm dirty, smelly, drunk, half-awake, brain-dead. There is virtually nothing lovable about me. But Jesus sees something entirely different. He sees me for who I am—His child.

Why is it so hard to accept this? I guess it'd be easier to accept if Jesus would just put on a physical disguise and find me, just like He found that homeless man outside the Fred Jordan Mission.

Too Much Noise

My world is filled with noise. The television is almost always on. When I get in my car, I turn up the radio. When I run on the treadmill, I turn on the television sets in the gym—not just one, but two. There are few moments in the day for thoughts of my own, and I don't like that.

It hasn't always been this way. In fact, during our separation, my wife wouldn't allow me back until I agreed to unplug the television—permanently. We lived for more than two years without a television set, only occasionally dragging it out of the closet to watch some big event.

Two years after Sara had unplugged the television, I arrived home to find her gone—along with much of the furniture. I soon realized that the television was gone as well. Suddenly, the silence that I had grown accustomed to was so loud that I needed something to drown it out, so my parents gave me an old television set.

In a way, the television was comforting. Having a baseball game on in the background while I tried to make out a check—the simplest of tasks being almost unbearable in those first few weeks after Sara left—somehow helped. But it soon became a crutch. The mindless chattering of the television set would quell the internal work that I needed to do. It would silence the painful memories that I needed to sort through and come to terms with.

I have recently become aware of this, yet I've done little to find more quiet time. I never have the immediate desire to be quiet—to understand who I really am behind the sports updates, the songs, and the phone calls. The desire to pray or to think or to read great books only comes in brief spurts.

The late Mike Yaconelli wrote about the need for "clearings," which give us time to get in touch with who we really are. Yaconelli described a clearing as "a place of shelter, peace, rest, safety, quiet, and healing. It is a place where you get your bearings, regroup, inspect the damage, fill out the estimate and make the repairs. It is the place where the mid-course corrections are made ... a clearing is a place where you can see what you couldn't see and hear what you couldn't hear."[1]

Yaconelli also wrote, "Clearings are not optional. They are longings in disguise. They are the required rest stops of life when our exhausted souls run out of steam ... If we don't seek the clearings, then we will be brought to them forcibly in the form of a heart attack, illness, breakdown, anxiety attack, depression and/or loneliness."[2]

The other day I was determined to be quiet, determined to eat dinner with the television off. I had been reading a book called *The Sacred Way* by Tony Jones. It talks about ancient spiritual disciplines that Christians have traditionally practiced, but today often neglect. One of those practices struck a cord: silence.

As I ate alone, without the television or radio on, I began to realize that I wasn't afraid of the silence anymore. It felt safe, like an ancient longing in disguise. And as the silence surrounded me—covered me—I realized that a clearing was just what I needed. As much as I wanted to run from it, I realized that Yaconelli was right: A clearing is not optional. If I hadn't found it, it would've found me.

So what did I learn from my time of silence? Things I can't express, things I can't put into words, things that felt a lot like healing.

Wash Over Me

Ever since New Year's Eve, pain has been washing over me like waves. Sometimes the waves are small, almost inconsequential; other times they're big enough to knock me down. January is a time to let go of the old and embrace the new, or so the Hallmark cards say. But I'm just starting to realize how far I am from escaping the past, from escaping my pain.

I'm not sure how I made it through Christmas without feeling these waves. I suppose that New Year's is different; it's nostalgic—the holiday where you are supposed to kiss someone at midnight. Pain becomes palpable when your wife is no longer there to kiss.

The other night I called a friend and asked if I could come over. She said yes, and we sat on her couch and made small talk and watched a made-for-TV movie. But our time together was awkward. I could hardly think of anything to say, and after about two hours, I finally grabbed my coat and said a hurried goodbye. Back in my car, weaving through deserted streets, I hit the "scan" button on the radio and found a Smashing Pumpkins song. Turning up the volume, I welcomed the painful wailing of Billy Corgan's voice. I blankly stared at the road—almost white from crushed winter salt—as the song washed over me.

I didn't hear the words, but I felt the emotion behind the words. And as I did, I instantly began thinking clearly. I realized why I had gone to my friend's house. I had gone there to forget Sara, to dull my pain, to remember how it felt to be wanted. But I didn't feel wanted. I didn't fit; my friend didn't fit.

I wanted the impossible: I wanted this friend to replace Sara. I wanted her to be everything Sara was and everything Sara wasn't. I wanted her to tell me that something was wrong with Sara; I wanted her to tell me that everything was right with me. I wanted her to breathe life into me. I wanted her to understand me, but she didn't.

What I really wanted was Sara. I wanted to smell her again. I wanted her to laugh at my jokes again. I wanted her to say she missed me. I wanted her to admit her faults, her sins, her errors. I wanted her to love me. I wanted her to hug me. I wanted to dream about us.

I'm trying to draw some sort of spiritual lesson from the emptiness that I feel, and the frustrating part is that maybe there isn't one. Or maybe there is, and I'm just too human, too earthbound to understand it.

Maybe the only way to make sense of life is to look at it through the eyes of Jesus, to feel life as Jesus felt it. Recently at church, I took Communion. "This is my body, which is broken for you," the woman at the front of the church said as she offered me the bread. "This is my blood, which is shed for you," the older man said, as he offered me the cup, repeating the words that Jesus said to His disciples on the night He was betrayed.

As I took the bread and the cup, I meditated on how Jesus was beaten and killed for my sake, how He was humiliated for my sake. He felt the pain of every divorce, every murder, every evil deed as He hung on the cross. And as He died, Jesus said, "Father, into your hands I commit my spirit" (Luke 23:46).

As I took Communion, I closed my eyes as His bones crunched between my teeth, as His blood soothed my parched throat. "Yes, Father. Into Your hands I commit my spirit. Make me a living sacrifice. Make me less of myself. Make me more of You. And as You do, help me find the person that I really am—the person created in Your image, unique and beautiful, full and complete, even without Sara."

True Beauty

The strangest thing happened one day at work. I experienced beauty—beauty in its truest sense, beauty as a gut-wrenching longing, beauty as a type of sadness. The kind of beauty that you find when you least expect it, the kind of beauty you experience when you're on your face praying and you look up and see a stranger, hand on your shoulder, praying over you. The kind of beauty you experience when you're searching for someone to love you, but instead you find someone to love—someone who can't love you back.

This kind of beauty is always unexpected, like when I walked into a coworker's office. He wasn't there, but when I looked up, there was a long window through which I could see a grove of trees. Covered in ice and snow, they looked like crystal unicorns. Some bowed and kissed the ground, others stretched upward, branches extended in gratitude.

I waited for someone to walk in and break the silence, but no one did. So I stood there stunned, transfixed, as if I were hovering over the grove. Suddenly beauty was all that mattered—not beauty for beauty's sake, but beauty as a manifestation of something holy, something unspoken, like the spirit of God hovering over the earth, about to create. In that moment, part of me died—the noisy, restless part—and there was just silence and peace and warmth, a warmth that felt like love and longing and sadness all at once.

As I looked on the scene, I felt alone. I was acutely aware that my wife was gone. Sara was not waiting to hear about beauty.

So impulsively, I took two steps, grabbed the phone, and called my friend Leslie, who worked in my department. I asked her to come to our coworker's office. I prayed that she would know about beauty, and something told me that she did.

We stood there, speechless. After a moment, she pointed to the low-hanging branches. She talked about being in the city, yet being in the middle of nature. She seemed to feel the same things that I did: sadness, happiness, longing. And after a moment of awe-filled silence, she said that the image of the magical trees was forever seared in her mind.

I told her that I needed someone to share the moment with, someone to validate the beauty that I saw. It was as if I were standing on holy ground, viewing something from another universe, and I needed a witness.

I am forever grateful that Leslie came and witnessed that beautiful scene.

But I needed more than that.

I needed someone to witness that I lived, that I experienced beauty. I needed someone to tell me that I mattered, that what I felt mattered, that what I experienced mattered. I needed someone to witness how badly I was hurting.

Something about beauty tells me that my hurt, my sadness, is simply the other side of happiness—they are two sides of the same coin. Perhaps sadness is a sort of beauty in itself. Perhaps there is something beautiful about being wounded because it teaches you to drink deeper and love deeper and stand at windows when you should be working and take deep breaths and consider leaving everything to find something else—something better, something holy, something beautiful.

My Anger Surfaces

It is strange how at peace with my divorce I sometimes am ... and then I have a moment like the night when my brother and I were playing tennis on vacation in Florida. Our match was proceeding nicely until I lost a game on a poor serve. Suddenly, like a madman, I hit a tennis ball far into the night sky. I then proceeded to slam my racket onto the court. It bounced several times before coming to a rest.

As I left to find the ball, I realized that my angry display was more than a typical reaction to a poor serve, and I think my brother realized it, too. Walking back to the lit court—wayward ball in hand—I looked up at my brother, who was suddenly quiet and withdrawn. We played several more games—but with noticeably less energy. And then the stadium lights went dark. The timer had expired. "Do you want to go back to the condo?" I asked as I found myself standing in darkness. He nodded.

We walked through dark streets lined with palm trees. We looked at the stars. We were quiet. I felt horrible. I wanted to explain something to my brother. I wanted to say, "Life didn't turn out the way I thought it would." But I couldn't manage the words.

Thinking about my outburst, I realized how much anger I still felt. For the first time since Sara left, I sensed a rage lurking just beneath the surface, a rage that could explode at any moment for any reason. And that scared me.

Forty Bags Have to Go

"Ladies and gentlemen, we have a weight problem—a balance issue—and we need to pull forty bags from the plane," the captain said over the intercom.

The plane, bound for Detroit, sat on a runway in Fort Myers, Florida, passengers bristling and cursing and peering through small windows as forty bags streamed down a conveyer belt and onto a small transport vehicle.

"They've got my bag!" someone yelled.

"I'm never riding this airline again," another passenger said.

I watched the conveyer belt spit out my blue duffel bag, and as it did, I slunk down into my seat, closing my eyes. The woman next to me was not so calm. Her sunburned face turned an even deeper shade of red as she saw her bag ejected from the plane. "I've got my medication in there! I've got my checkbook in there!"

She started to curse airline employees under her breath. "I live in Toledo," she said. "I don't know how the hell I'm going to get my bag." Other passengers were just as irate—they roamed the aisles, talking with no small degree of agitation about the unexpected turn of events.

A flight attendant finally got on the intercom, imploring people to sit down. "We cannot take off until everyone is in their seats," she said. "Please sit down." Within a few minutes, the flight crew had regained control of the plane, and soon we were in the air. The impending passenger revolt was put down without major incident.

I couldn't help thinking about those forty bags, about how hard it is to accept those things in life that are out of our control. No one on the plane deserved to have their bags left behind; no one deserved to be inconvenienced. But they were.

Sometimes, no matter how well we plan, our bags get thrown off the plane, and we're forced to deal with the repercussions. I guess the only thing we can control is how we react. Will we curse and yell and get angry or will we exhale and lean back and allow God to work out the details?

As I write this, it's been about ten hours since the plane landed, and I'm still waiting for my luggage. But something tells me God will work out the details. And if He doesn't, that will be okay, too. I just wish I felt this way all the time.

Hollywood Divorce

I recently read an article about John Stamos, the actor famous for his role on *Full House*. His marriage to model Rebecca Romijn ended in divorce, and like most Hollywood stars, Stamos gave the breakup a positive spin. He told a reporter, "My relationship was really fun. We had a great time. Maybe too much fun."

Brad Pitt and Jennifer Aniston also went through a very public divorce. But to my amazement, they issued a cheery statement about how they planned to remain close friends.

And the other day as I walked out of my favorite bookstore, a gossip magazine's headline proclaimed something called "The Happy Divorce."

This sort of thing makes me angry. Maybe I'm old-fashioned,

but I have trouble understanding how divorce is anything but painful. In my estimation, "The Happy Divorce" is akin to "The Pleasurable Cancer Radiation Treatment."

I wonder if downplaying the pain of divorce leads many people to believe that divorce isn't that big of a deal, that those of us who are divorced should just "get over it" and "move on," that divorce has few side effects, that divorce can even be "happy."

Obviously, I'm not John Stamos or Brad Pitt because I'm not happy to be divorced. Sara and I are not close friends. Our failed marriage is not a fond memory. Our divorce was not "mutual" or "cordial" or "happy." My marriage was never intended as a warm-up for something better. It was for life. And now it's over.

An Empty Mattress

Sara and I were very cautious with our money. One of the biggest purchases we made was a mattress. At the time, it seemed expensive—at least for two Christian school employees. But when we found the perfect mattress, queen-sized with pillow-top padding, we decided to buy it. We had done our research and knew that we were getting a good deal even if it was expensive.

I remember the purchase with sad fondness; I recall Sara going into the mattress store on the first day of every month with a check. She wasn't about to let them charge us interest. The store clerk would shake his head and smile as Sara walked through the door with our payment, right on time.

When Sara left and filed for divorce, she took several pieces of furniture with her, but she left the mattress behind—the mattress that she so diligently paid for each month.

As I lie alone on that same pillow-top mattress, I sometimes think of Sara's faithfulness in paying for it, of the times Sara and I sat on the mattress and talked, of the times we tenderly held each other. I remember watching her sleep, her pink night-gown-covered shoulders methodically rising and falling with each breath.

I see her light brown hair tucked behind her ears, her rose lips slightly agape. I smell her skin—a mixture of face wash and moisturizer and whatever it was that was distinctly her. I see her folding her reading glasses up and placing them in a brown plastic case—I can actually hear the snap of the case as she closes it, and I can see her setting the case in the nightstand drawer just before she turns off the light.

All of these memories come rushing back as I lie on our mattress. Most nights, I'm too tired, too preoccupied to let the memories come. But some nights I let my guard down, and when I do, the memories blow through the room like a late autumn wind. And when the wind blows, I feel sad and cold. I utter nonsense prayers:

> God, I'm so lonely. I'm just lying here, think-
> ing about Sara. I feel so sad. I just pray that she
> will come back ... love me again, but I know
> that's probably not what I want, or probably
> not what I need. I don't know. I don't know
> what to pray. I guess I'm just praying that Your
> will be done ... whatever that is. I guess I'm just
> praying that maybe someone will come into
> my life—a woman—someone to love. I know
> I probably have stuff to deal with first before
> that can happen. And You know part of me still

loves Sara. But it looks like she's never coming back ... and I think I can deal with that ...
well, at least most of the time, but maybe not
tonight. I need Your help tonight. Please help.

Usually after praying something like this, I'll tuck a pillow
under my arm and fall asleep, not really sure whether God will
answer my prayer or not. It's a big mattress to sleep on alone,
but I'm learning to stretch into the empty spaces.

Shoebox of Memories

I procrastinated as long as I could. I walked around my apartment, looking for things to clean. I thought about calling a
friend, thought about going to the gym, thought about watching television. But in the end, I knew that I had to work on this
chapter.

I didn't feel like writing it because I didn't want to hurt, and
something told me that writing this section would feel like
ripping a bandage off a freshly scabbed wound. But I had to do
it—not only because I had to finish this chapter, but because
the only way around pain is to walk straight through it. And
there was seemingly no more direct route than the one I was
about to take: immersing myself in memories, in words that
turned out to be lies, in photographs of smiling faces that would
never again smile for my camera.

I picked up the shoebox from the table and brought it to the
couch. Placing it at my feet, I began pulling out letters and
photos. Sara had saved nearly every keepsake from our relationship. There were letters that we wrote to each other as college
freshmen. There were ticket stubs from theater performances.
There were Valentine's Day cards, including one that Sara gave

me less than five months before she left. There were pictures of us on the beach or in front of the Grand Canyon. There was a postcard I sent her six years ago from Montreal. There were Post-It notes with scribbled messages: "Love you—can't wait for tonight! Forever, S." These messages were the saddest—in some ways even sadder than the pictures.

"I can't wait to see what the Lord will do in our relationship," Sara wrote inside one card. Or another: "I know God has wonderful plans in store for us ... you have my heart now and forever."

One letter even acknowledged things I had forgotten Sara ever said or wrote. Sara admitting that she was sometimes "difficult." Sara thanking me for helping her around the house. Sara acknowledging—days before our first wedding anniversary—that despite our problems, she loved being married to me.

I sat on the couch and blankly read the notes. I thought that the shoebox might be more therapeutic. I thought that I might cry, that I might gain profound insights, that something might happen. But nothing did.

I didn't have any startling revelations; there was no emotional outburst. There was just sadness—deep, chronic sadness. And still, no tears. It had been so long since I had cried. When would it come? What would it take?

It would take more than finding a blank card with a long piece of Sara's hair stuck to it. It would take more than a photograph of Sara and me laughing, tickling each other. It would take more than a copy of the speech that my best man gave at our wedding.

Maybe it will just take time. A friend of mine was once diagnosed with terminal cancer. Months of chemical treatments and prayers and even a trip to a healing service produced no relief. He was prepared to die—anxious to be with his Creator at last—when unexpectedly his cancer was gone. Doctors were confused. He was confused. And it wasn't until many months later that he finally cried.

I can relate to his story because I didn't cry the day my wife left. I wanted to, but no tears came. I didn't cry on Christmas Day. I thought I might, but I felt fine. I didn't even cry on New Year's Eve when I felt completely empty.

And now, more than eight months after Sara left, I'm still dry-eyed, still straight-faced, still wondering what it will take to unleash the dam of pain. I want to sprinkle the dry ground of my heart with tears. I want something to grow there again, but right now there are only dead things. My heart is the texture of a desert floor, cracked and dry, in need of moisture and healing—waiting for living things to crawl out from sun-scorched places.

One of the last letters I read before I closed the shoebox was a note from Sara's mother, one that I'm not sure I had ever read before. It said:

> Sara,
>
> I always read the verse on top of the bookcase in your room every day when I make the bed. Today's made me think of me and dad, with our anniversary being tomorrow. It also made me think of you and Cameron. I looked at

> the picture of the two of you in the sunflower
> frame ... did you ever notice what kind of eyes
> he has? He has a gentle soul. It made me stop
> and thank God that you found one another ...

I folded the letter up and placed it back in the shoebox. I closed the shoebox and shook my head. Sara's parents are now divorced; Sara and I are now divorced.

I went to bed. I felt incredibly sad.

I didn't cry.

The Glass Menagerie

I sometimes wonder if I feel sad for no reason other than I like feeling sad. I wonder if my sadness has become a part of me, a weight that would feel strange to no longer carry.

I have things to legitimately be sad about, but what about healing? What about closure? What about the idea that healing can happen, should happen? But I first have to let it happen. Maybe I'm just not ready to let go. Maybe I'm not ready to begin living and feeling and breathing like everyone else. I think I'll recover—I think I'm starting to—but perhaps not as quickly as I would like. Broken things take varying amounts of time to heal—be they hands or legs or spirits. But I wonder if I have unknowingly slowed the healing process because when I feel sad, I feel special, deep, mysterious, and creative. I feel as if I am separate from the rest of the world. This is both horrible and strangely addictive.

It reminds me of Tennessee Williams' play, *The Glass Menagerie*, in which the main character, Laura, is as fragile as her glass animal figurines—her glass menagerie. Laura has trouble entering into the real world, in part because she walks with a limp. Laura and her family allow the ailment to make her not only physically fragile, but emotionally fragile as well.

Laura's fragility is what makes her as special as her glass menagerie. Laura is unwilling, or unable, to move beyond the pain and join the rest of society, to leave the shelf of her glass menagerie. Laura's story makes me think about my situation. It makes me wonder whether I might become trapped in a state of emotional infancy, trapped on the shelf.

I recently met a beautiful woman who I'll call Hope. I seem to connect with Hope on a deep level. She seems to be one of those kindred spirits. But as much as I would like to pursue a relationship with her, I first need to make sure that my soul is healed—my heart is healed—at least as much as it ever will be. I wrote a poem called "A Writer's Date" for Hope, and after she read it, she knew that I was not quite ready. After I wrote it, I knew that I was not quite ready. But for the first time since Sara left, I was determined to not become a glass monument to sadness. I was determined to leave the shelf.

A Writer's Date

A table for two.
Candlelight.
A glowing screen.
The flicker of rainwater.
A flame to keep us warm.

Puddles outside, but inside, words dry up.

Tonight it is only you
Sitting across from me
Telling me to write something else
Telling me to save the sad stories for another time

I protest, but not too much.

Tonight, the sad stories will wait.
Tonight, the rain will dry our tears.
Tonight, the words will flood.

And they will belong only to you.

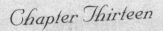

Chapter Thirteen

Evil, Love, and Grace

The more you know, the less you feel
Some pray for, others steal
Blessings are not just for the ones who kneel ... luckily

—"City of Blinding Lights," U2

I was eight years old when I first learned about evil. I was playing in the backyard with my best friend Carol, who lived in the
neighborhood behind my house.

One day, Carol and I began arguing when suddenly my hand,
seemingly of its own accord, flew up and hit her in the face. It
was a backhanded slap that was noiseless, thoughtless. I was a
quiet child, often complimented by adults for my maturity and
good behavior, so I was shocked when I realized what I had
done. The memory is forever with me: Carol screaming, run-

ning across my backyard toward her house holding her mouth, blood on her hands, loose teeth, me standing there in complete disbelief hardly able to comprehend what I had just done.

It was at that moment that I realized I was capable of hurting others, capable of doing something evil. And like Adam and Eve hiding from God after eating the forbidden fruit, I climbed a tree and hid, ashamed. I knew something was wrong.

Soon, my mom came outside looking for me. Hearing whimpers from the branches of the tree, she coaxed me down, and I talked to her through bursts of tears. I must have told her what I had done, but I don't remember what I said. I just remember drawing a picture for Carol and writing an apology on it, which I sheepishly handed to Carol's father some time after the incident. Unfortunately, it didn't do much good.

Carol's parents never let her see me again, which I suppose isn't that surprising. Sometimes you don't get a second chance. Sometimes people don't trust you again. Sometimes you can't make amends. But the good news is this: Grace wins. Or as a bumper sticker proclaims: Love Wins. Love wins because Jesus died and came to life again. Love wins because we have a shot at redemption. Love wins because, as the political revolutionary on the cross, Jesus invites people like us, imperfect people, to join Him in paradise, to join Him in the city of blinding lights: "Blessings are not just for the ones who kneel," sings U2.

But while love ultimately wins, it doesn't always win here on earth. In fact, more often than not, love loses. A spouse leaves after years of counseling and praying. A child dies after a long battle with cancer. An African village is wiped out by AIDS. A gun battle erupts. A despondent mother kills herself. Armies march. Bombs drop. Evil and disease win, at least for a season.

The great writer and philosopher C.S. Lewis wrote in *The Problem of Pain* that the history of humankind is "largely a record of crime, war, disease, and terror, with just sufficient happiness interposed to give [humans], while it lasts, an agonized apprehension of losing it, and, when it is lost, the poignant misery of remembering."[1]

I suppose that's what makes evil so painful: We know of something better. Even as an eight-year-old, I knew of something better—I knew of times when Carol and I laughed, times when we watched television together, times when we played hide-and-seek.

And as I stood there with blood on my hands after slapping Carol, I was left with ancient memories, with the vague idea that things were no longer as they once were. Evil became a very real part of my life; it looked me in the face and challenged me to a fight.

It is the same evil that my wife first confronted me with years ago, evil that manifested itself in lies and lust and selfishness. These things were lobbed at me like grenades, which made me want to run before they exploded, to climb a tree and hide, just as I had as an eight-year-old. I didn't want to face the ugly reality that I was still capable of evil.

You see, I have the imprint of God on me. I am good. I am beautiful. I am made by the Creator. But I am also cursed. This is the horrible tension that I live with, the horrible tension that you live with: On top of the beautiful painting are messy marks of ugly charcoal, all but blotting out the masterpiece underneath. And only love, wearing the glasses of grace, can begin to see through the scribbles.

"What causes fights and quarrels among you?" the biblical writer James once asked. "Don't they come from your desires that battle within you? You want something but don't get it. You kill and covet, but you cannot have what you want. You quarrel and fight" (James 4:1-2).

If James is right, then what are we supposed to do with the fact that we are less like superheroes and more like antiheroes, less like Superman and more like our fathers and mothers, capable of great good and great evil.

I don't know, and I don't think I'm supposed to know. However, I do know this: The Bible is filled with holy screwups. The Scriptures say that David was a man after God's own heart, yet he committed adultery and killed a man to cover up the affair. Rahab was a prostitute, yet she was part of the lineage of Jesus and is commended in the Bible for helping Israelite spies escape. Abraham gave his wife over to another man to avoid getting killed. Peter lied three times about even knowing Jesus after spending years at His side.

Maybe you and I can be holy screwups, maybe we can add ourselves to this list, maybe with all our inconsistencies, all our imperfections, all our evil, there's something that God can salvage.

Love Is All We Need

One of the amazing things about being human is this: We all need to be needed, regardless of who we are or what we have done. We have lost respect for ourselves, we have lost our dignity, we have lost a loved one, we have lost our ability to cope with life. We all have a dark hole of despair that needs to be filled with companionship and love.

As C.S. Lewis said, "If He who in Himself can lack nothing chooses to need us, it is because we need to be needed."[2] If He requires love, then how much more will we?

But love poses a problem: It's hard. Love may be the answer, but it's not an easy answer. If you don't believe me, try loving the next person who cuts you off in traffic. Try loving the person who spreads rumors about you at work. Try loving the spouse who leaves you with no warning, no forwarding address, and no desire to ever see you again.

Love is a topic addressed throughout the Scriptures. Jesus said there is no greater love than the love of one who lays down his life for his friends (John 15:13). I wonder if the love and connection that we all long for is only found in living in community with one another and with Jesus, who lay down His life for His friends.

The Song of Grace: The Song of Bastards

In Sunday school I learned that grace was "unmerited favor," something that you don't deserve but receive anyway. Perhaps an even better definition of grace is recorded in Philip Yancey's book *What's So Amazing About Grace?*

In the book, Yancey relates the story of Will Campbell, a pastor and professor. Challenged by an agnostic friend to define the entire Christian message in ten words or less, Campbell said: "We're all bastards, but God loves us anyway."[3]

We are all bastards, not only in the truest sense of the word—illegitimate children "adopted" by God—but bastards in the crass sense—unlovable, irritating, and pitiful.

As much as I appreciate Campbell's definition of the Christian message—which, in essence, is the definition of grace—I don't think you ever truly learn what grace is until you experience it, until you need it so badly that you would give anything for it.

In some ways, I am still searching for grace.

Why? Because in the words of Yancey, there is also something called "ungrace," an attitude fueled by anger and resentment, an attitude that refuses to release the guilty party of his or her guilt. I experienced more than two years of ungrace from my wife, and if I'm honest, I must admit that she experienced much ungrace from me as well.

In her mind, I was unforgivably guilty of sticking up for my parents instead of sticking up for her, for fantasizing about other women, for not cherishing her, for not loving her as I should have. This resentment grew like a parasite in her soul, to the point that she could hardly stand to look at me. Instead of seeing me through the eyes of grace—seeing the beautiful painting that I was underneath—she could only see the ugly charcoal smudges. She couldn't remember that underneath the filth I was wonderfully made by a creative God; that deep down I was something good, something worthy, a child of God—albeit an adopted one.

In addition she was too hurt to see that she was also marred by the evil that infects all of us. Her pain defined her; her pain became her reality. I was the cause of that pain, so the solution was simple. To stop the pain, she must remove herself from its source.

I'd like to point the finger at her, but I can't. Her reaction is all too consistent with my own. Most of us give grace about as

generously as we give money. It's because grace is unfair. Grace
is seeing that "justice" is not carried out, and that grates on us.
In fact, everything within us screams in protest because we like
to see people punished.

So did the people in Jesus' day, which is why they wanted to
throw stones at the woman caught in adultery. And yet look at
what Jesus did: He said, "If any one of you is without sin, let
him be the first to throw a stone at her" (John 8:7). One by one,
the men left. Grace. No punishment meted out to the guilty.
Jesus simply asked her, "Woman, where are they? Has no one
condemned you?" "No one, sir," she said. "Then neither do I
condemn you," Jesus declared. "Go now and leave your life of
sin" (John 8:10-11).

Yancey makes the profound statement in his book that "there is
nothing we can do to make God love us more. There is nothing we can do to make God love us less."[4] And this story of the
woman caught in adultery proves his point.

I finally realize that I too have experienced grace; I was just
looking for it in the wrong place. Right now, I hear Jesus saying
to me, "Then neither do I condemn you." I hear Jesus saying to
me, "Go now and leave your life of sin." And somehow I feel
changed—because that's what grace does. It compels us to love.
It compels us to change. Not through force, but through a sense
of undying gratitude at having been given another chance, a
chance that we didn't deserve, a chance extended to bastards
like you and me.

Crime and Punishment

In Dostoyevsky's classic novel *Crime and Punishment*, a college
dropout named Raskolnikov—depressed, out of work, and

deeply in debt—begins to fantasize about killing a loathsome old woman who makes her living as a moneylender.

Virtually cut off from the outside world, Raskolnikov begins to talk to himself, practically stops eating, and starts avoiding other people. He begins having fevers. He begins thinking more and more about killing the old moneylender to the point of actually planning how he would commit the murder. One day he finds himself on a "dress rehearsal" for the murder, figuring out how long it would take him to get to the old woman's apartment, observing who might be around when he kills, and plotting his escape route.

He tries to laugh off the whole thing as nonsense, but deep down he knows that he has already crossed the line between fantasy and reality. He knows that he is going to murder the old woman, for no other reason than he can, for no other reason than he wants to prove that he is made of extraordinary stuff, the stuff that geniuses are made of, the stuff that Napoleon was made of.

Raskolnikov wants to prove that he is not bound by the moral constraints of ordinary humans. He figures that he will not suffer the consequences of his horrible deed because he is above the ordinary, above the moral and social laws of the universe.

Raskolnikov does kill the old woman, and in an unplanned turn of events, also ends up killing the old woman's daughter. The rest of the novel is a study in psychology and sin, as Raskolnikov begins to hunt the police almost as much as they begin to hunt him. Terrified at the thought of being discovered, yet at the same time attracted to justice like a fly to bright light, Raskolnikov takes stupid, unnecessary risks, giving away clues about the murder to the police and others.

Finally, Raskolnikov meets a young woman who is a prostitute. She sells her body in order to support her mother and young siblings who are virtually penniless due to her father's drinking. And for some reason, Raskolnikov stops his charade and tells this woman, Sonya, about the murders. Sonya, a devout Christian, then does something unexpected: She cries. She mourns for Raskolnikov. She holds him. And she encourages him to turn himself in but promises that if he does, she will follow him. In some strange way she sees herself as irrevocably connected to Raskolnikov. Sonya won't turn her back on Raskolnikov. She hates what he has done, but she loves him.

Sonya is grace personified. Sonya is a Christ figure. And through her love, Raskolnikov is redeemed. In fact, the novel ends as Raskolnikov, released from prison after several years of hard labor, is on his knees next to Sonya, crying.

I finished this book shortly after my wife left. And I realized that I wanted Sonya. I wanted grace. I wanted someone to hear my sins, my faults, my confessions, and I wanted someone to weep for me. I wanted someone to love me. I wanted someone to forgive me, to express the inexpressible, to express the love that Jesus always showed those He came in contact with, the kind of love that Sonya expressed to Raskolnikov.

Sonya

A whore
With
Her
Hair

Down.

Bangs

Over

Her
Eyes.

Nervous
Hands
Stained with
Wine.

Afraid to
Look.

But look at me!

I too am broken.
I too am ashamed.
I too know demons.

So let us carry our sins together
Let us walk up the hill with heavy loads
Let us tear out our eyes, pierce our lips
Cut our hands with
Ice.

Let us confess
What can only be
Whispered.

Let us remember,

We are dead
We are dead
We are dead

Let us forget who we are, if we ever knew

Let us say we are the right kind of people

Let us remember how it feels

To be

Naked

And

Unashamed.

Let us begin by ending.

And you,

Sonya,
Will say prayers
For our journey.

And they will be enough.

Gravity and Grace

Every day I think about my ex-wife, and everyday I disagree
with what she did. Every day I disagree with how she left. Some
days, I feel angry. But every day I must try to picture how much

Jesus has done for me and remember that I am the recipient of His grace. And as I come to understand this and, perhaps more importantly, feel this, I will be more and more able to extend that kind of grace to others, including my ex-wife.

Offering her grace will take some doing, some time, something holy. It will take all of these things, because she doesn't deserve it. And that's exactly the point.

Chapter Fourteen

Visitation

My hands are tied, my body bruised
She got me with nothing to win
And nothing else to lose

—"With or Without You," U2

It had been a long day at work, and I was exhausted. It was only six o'clock, but it was already dark outside as I pulled into the parking lot of my apartment building. As I approached the covered parking area, I saw a red car parked near the door to my apartment. I slowed my car to a crawl, staring at the red car's license plate in horror, as if I were watching a car wreck in slow motion. Pulling into my parking spot, the first three letters of the car's license plate ran through my head. I was trying to convince myself that it wasn't her, but it was. I couldn't believe it.

I took the keys out of the ignition and stared at the red car through my rearview mirror.

My heart pounded.

The ghost had come to visit.

I wanted to run away. I wanted to walk straight into my apartment and ignore her. I wanted to set sail for a faraway island—a million miles from darkness, a million miles from winter, a million miles from pain.

I grabbed my briefcase and laptop and climbed out of the car. I felt as if I might start shaking at any moment. I closed the car door and walked toward my apartment, looking over at the red car, wondering if anyone was in there. I felt half-alive, as if marching toward my grave, a skeleton of myself.

I could hear my footsteps echo across the parking lot.

As I approached the front door to the apartment building—now fumbling with my keys—a small figure emerged from the red car. It was her, but she looked different. Her face looked pale, even ghostly, her hair shorter than I had ever seen it—shorter than mine. She looked older; she looked like her mother. It was as if the pain of living had physically changed her. She looked like she needed something so badly, but had no idea what it was she needed.

And for the first time since she left, I felt badly for her.

She stood behind the car looking at me. The cold December air shot through my body, and I clenched my hands and put them in my coat pockets. For a few moments, we just looked at each other. The pain, the hurt, the longing were tangible. She had the look of a wounded animal.

"I shouldn't have come here, but I wanted to ask you something," she said.

Her voice was difficult to hear, and I instinctively craned my neck closer to her.

"Okay," I said.

In that moment, I didn't miss her. I suddenly remembered all of the bad things—all the yelling, all the pain, all the anger—and I wanted to run away. I wanted to be anywhere but standing in that parking lot, looking at her.

But I still cared about her. I still wanted to help her—to love her, to hug her, to try again—but deep down I knew that I couldn't. I could never love her enough. There was something broken inside of her that I couldn't fix, something that only Jesus could fix. It was frightening just standing there. It seemed as if she had the power to condemn me to hell, as if she could hurt me again. I kept a bubble of nearly ten feet between us. I didn't want her to come any closer—I was too scared of what she might do.

"I came here to ask you a question," she said, still standing behind her car.

"Okay," I said.

"In your email, you said you were writing a book. Would this book have anything to do with me?"

I paused and thought about whether I should answer.

"It's none of my business, but if it's about me, I'd like to know," she added.

"Maybe," I said. "I mean, I haven't written it yet, but it will be about my life, so yes, you will be in it. But I will protect your identity—I'm not trying to hurt you by writing a book."

"It's one thing if you want to write about yourself, but when you pull me into it, it just seems like it would be really biased— I guess it would have to be since you're the only one writing it. But I would just want you to be really careful," she said. "I have always been really careful about telling people about you— about us. There are just some things that are so personal."

It struck me as odd that she was saying these things. It seemed as if she were terrified of how she might appear in the book. It struck me that she had finally realized that there were things that she should be ashamed of, things for which she had never apologized.

"The book will be biased, I mean, it must be. Everything is viewed through my eyes, through my experiences. But if anything, I will come out looking worse than you do," I said. "I'm not afraid to put it all out there, to show the worst of myself."

"Well, that's fine," she said. "But I just want you to be careful with what you share about me ... I just hope that you'll think really seriously about this before writing it."

It seemed as if she could talk about the book for hours. But I was quiet, stoic, and she sensed my reticence to talk. So she apologized for coming. She couldn't help it; she had to come. She had to know about the book, she said.

And for a moment, the conversation came to a halt. We just stood there, looking at each other. For a brief moment it was just the two of us—the same two souls that were joined as husband and wife in holy matrimony, the same two souls that had said, "I do ... for better or for worse ... till death do us part," staring into each other's eyes.

"New coat?" she finally asked.

As she said it, she smiled. She smiled.

In that moment, I saw the girl I fell in love with. I remembered laughing together, only nineteen years old, but happy. I was transported back to warm afternoons, dreaming about life—afternoons when nothing seemed impossible. In memory, I still see spring days on college lawns, arms touching, kissing. I still see days that seemed as if they would never end, as if they were only the beginning of a million warm days together.

And now here we were talking about divorce. Our divorce.

Here we were, standing in a dark parking lot, hundreds of arguments from "Will you marry me?"

Even writing this makes me want to rip out my heart. I don't want to feel because it hurts too much. I want to scream at Jesus and ask Him why He didn't help when I was on my knees praying for Him to change me, to change my circumstances, to heal my marriage. But then I realize that Jesus should scream at me for all of the things I've never done, scream at me for being so short-sighted, scream at me for thinking that my will must be His will.

"There's one more thing I'd like to ask you, but it's none of my business, so I won't," Sara said. "Okay, maybe I will ... are you dating anyone? Again, it's none of my business ... it's just this book, and then I heard about you being somewhere with someone, and ... it's just a lot at once. I was just sort of taken aback by it all."

"Who saw me with someone? No, I'm not dating. I have friends that I've hung out with ... you don't even know the situation, and now you're asking this about me?" I asked.

"No, you're right, I don't, I don't know the situation," she said. "It just surprised me, that's all. I mean, it's only been six weeks since we've been divorced," she said.

"You mean six months?"

"Six weeks since it's been finalized," she said, rattling off a specific date.

"I wouldn't know," I said. "I didn't look at the papers—I had them sent to my dad. I didn't want to see them."

"I figured that you would need to be with someone. I'm just the opposite. I was at this Halloween party, and this guy came up to me, and ..."

"Sara, stop. Just stop. I don't need to hear this. I don't want to hear this—you and some other guy. Why are you telling me this?" I asked.

"I'm sorry, I'm sorry, I'm sorry—you're right—I'm sorry, I'm sorry," she said. She kept saying sorry. "I just don't understand how you can say in an email that you miss me and then be going out with other people," she added.

"Sara, you don't even know the situation. I'm not seeing anyone. I'm not dating. You don't even know what you're talking about."

"But all of those things you said in your email about missing me—why would you say that and then go out with other women?"

"I do miss you, but it's not like you're coming back, Sara. I don't know why you're here. This is just making me upset again. I don't want to feel like this," I said.

Tears started to form, but I held them back. I stared off into the distance.

"I'm sorry. I know, I shouldn't have come," Sara said. "No contact." But she made no attempt to leave, so I did.

"Well, you better go, and I better get inside," I said, clenching my hands, which stung from the cold air.

I started to walk toward my apartment door, but stopped and looked back at Sara. I nodded at her car. "You're in your old spot—or my old spot, where I used to park."

She said nothing.

I walked inside, filled with sadness and pain and love. I was also filled with resolve to live, resolve to try to find God, to see what He wanted and how I might be a part of Him and He a part of me.

Sara, I wish you could've made this journey with me, but you couldn't. Something inside wouldn't let you. But I forgive you. And I will live without you.

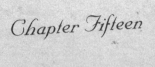

Chapter Fifteen

Day Three

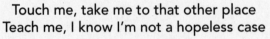

Touch me, take me to that other place
Teach me, I know I'm not a hopeless case

—"Beautiful Day," U2

This is not the part of the book where I tell you that everything is great. This is not the part of the book where I suggest that you can now dismiss all of the big, messy questions surrounding my divorce, your divorce, or your friend's or family member's divorce. But I can say that it's now been nearly one year since Sara left, and healing has taken place. Don't get me wrong, there are still days where I feel sad, still moments when I question.

But I rarely feel angry with Sara. I rarely feel like finding her. I no longer hope that she contacts me. I guess, in many ways, I have made my peace with Sara, because most days I feel as if I have forgiven her, which I can only attribute to Jesus. I am too human, too selfish to have forgiven Sara without some divine assistance.

In fact, I wonder if we can experience genuine forgiveness, genuine healing apart from Jesus. Perhaps we can, but there is one thing that only comes through Jesus: Day Three. On Day Three, Jesus walked away from death and toward the light of His Father. On Day Three, Jesus opened our eyes to a new reality: God is with us. God is present. God has spoken. God came to earth and showed us that there is more to this world than what we can see. God showed us that often the greatest realities are the invisible ones.

I wonder if divorce is less about walking away from something and more about walking toward something. Walking toward life with God, toward the life we have always been called to—a life of gratitude, a life of service, a life of God at the center, a life of "kingdom come on earth as it is in heaven."

It is tough to walk when everything feels dead. But what if death cannot hold me? What if death ultimately has no power over me, over you, over us? What if death's power is only temporary? What if we will lie in graves, but only for a time?

Death could not hold Jesus. Perhaps it cannot hold us either.

Perhaps after a time of testing and a time of sorrow, Day Three will come.

And when Day Three comes, we will leave our grave clothes behind. We will leave our mourning and walk into a new morning with him, a morning when our sorrows are turned to dancing. And we will dance like we have never danced before. We will dance with a joy that some will never know, a joy that only the brokenhearted know.

Today, after nine months, I cried. But tomorrow I will laugh. Tomorrow I will wipe away my tears. Tomorrow I will meet the Man in white. And He will say:

This is new birth.

This is heaven's light.

This is healing.

This is forgiveness.

This is redemption.

This is Day Three.

Notes

Preface

1. John Steinbeck, *Travels with Charley* (New York: Penguin Books, 1962) p. 152.

Chapter 1: The Shaky Beginning of a Dream

1. William Shakespeare, *The Complete Works* (Oxford: Oxford University Press, 1988) p. 754.

Chapter 3: Engagement

1. Erwin McManus, *The Barbarian Way* (Nashville, TN: Nelson Books, 2004) p. 88.
2. Ibid., p. 88–89.

Chapter 7: Losing Myself

1. William Shakespeare, *The Complete Works* (Oxford: Oxford University Press, 1988) p. 754.

Chapter 12: Wrestling with God and Demons

1. Mike Yaconelli, *Collected Writings* (El Cajon, CA: Youth Specialties, 2004) p. 101.
2. Ibid.

Chapter 13: Evil, Love, and Grace

1. C.S. Lewis, *The Problem of Pain* (New York: Simon & Schuster, 1996) p. 12.
2. Ibid., p. 45.
3. Philip Yancey, *What's So Amazing About Grace?* (Grand Rapids, MI: Zondervan, 1997) p. 142.
4. Ibid, p. 70.

All U2 song lyrics were taken from *www.U2.com*.